Introduction

If you picked up this book you likely are a parent or soon will be one. You probably care very much about the future of your children and wonder what you need to do to be a great parent. The key question you must ask yourself is how far are you willing to go? How much is too much to ask for giving your children the best possible start in life? Many parents would just about write a blank check if they could be guaranteed a positive outcome for their children.

What if how much time and energy you commit to spend with your children actually had far more effect on the outcome than any amount of money you could spend? How much time and effort would you be willing to put in if it could make the difference between self confident, independent and successful children versus kids that drift through life lacking confidence, guidance and direction? Why pay a stranger to watch your children, (really it's more like sit in the corner and send text messages) when what they really want – what they really need, is to know that you will be there for them – whenever they need you?

While your family circumstances may not allow you to be with your children twenty-four hours a day, what you can do is make the most of the time you can spend with them. If you or your spouse can stay at home I highly encourage you to consider it. You may need to put your career on hold for a while but if you dedicate yourself to using the skills and techniques laid out in this book, you can be assured you will have done everything possible to help your kids get a great start in life.

If you are already a parent, you already know how challenging a responsibility it can be, but what if most of these challenging times could be turned inside out? What if you looked at each frustrating moment and saw an opportunity to teach – yourself and your children – how to handle the situation in a better way the next time it comes up? One of the biggest secrets to developing good behavior skills is growing your children's understanding of the world and your attitude towards helping them learn about it.

What is parental leadership and why is it important to me?

Leadership could be defined in many different ways but one thing it clearly is NOT is automatic. Leadership isn't something you are born with; it must be learned, practiced and developed over time. For those that understand the concepts and have the courage to make changes in themselves, great things happen. Effective leadership is the one common thread in most of all great human achievements. Effective leaders inspire and motivate people to follow their visions willingly and eagerly, not out of fear. Their followers voluntarily challenge themselves to the goals the leader has established and diligently work hard everyday out of commitment to these goals, not because of demands for compliance.

A parent applying basic leadership skills to family life brings a common understanding of the family goals and what each member must do to ensure the family achieves these goals together. Establishing the vision of the family goals and helping kids learn to treat others (adults and children) the way they want to be treated are the foundation. Building a family plan with expectations and accountability for all members builds up the family and motivates each person to do their personal best everyday. With each family member working hard to do their best each day to help the family achieve the goals you have established, anything becomes possible.

Imagine having children that work hard towards carefully crafted goals and voluntarily contribute to the family. Imagine self-confident kids that speak up to ask logical questions, gather information, think for themselves, and then make good decisions on their own. Imagine healthy kids that are well adjusted, physically active, socially adept and treat everyone they meet with respect. Not only is it possible, it is likely to happen if you learn and practice leadership principles everyday.

Make no mistake, leadership is not acting the part, it is living the part. The vast majority of human communication is non-verbal. Your kids will understand how you really feel about something regardless of the words you use. They can interpret your body language better than anyone else in your life, because they are hardwired from birth to learn from their parents. It's what you do each day that tells the story of what is truly most important to you. Instead of pretending and offering "do as I say, not do as I do" lessons, you need to commit yourself to be the example of the lifestyle you are teaching your kids to choose for themselves.

The ability to explain the reasons why and then to demonstrate commitment to solid moral standards are the foundation of your credibility. Demonstrating your credibility through your daily actions is critical to earning trust. Remember that credibility and trust can be lost in a single incident so you must be consistent every day.

Earning the trust of your children may seem automatic for a parent, but this is not always the case. For your children to choose your example as their own chosen lifestyle, even while free to select other lifestyles, they must first choose to trust you. Next they must understand why you do the things you do. If you can explain the reasons why things are important and you consistently do what you say you will do you will be establishing your credibility. If you can consistently show you are worthy of their trust, they will listen and consider carefully everything you tell them. If you can do this, you and children will achieve whatever goals you commit to achieve.

What do I do next?

You may have already read several books on parenting but what you have not likely seen is how to use leadership techniques to connect with your child. Preparing kids for success in a challenging world requires commitment, hard work, and a positive attitude. A highly engaged parent with a positive attitude can help young children and even infants learn communication skills and develop a true understanding of their world. Combine a high level of understanding with proven effective structure and accountability processes and you can engage your children in a life-long passion for learning. Passionately engaged kids with an understanding of their world learn to develop self-confidence, ask great questions, as well as think and decide for themselves. It is through proficiency with using these tools (understanding, self confidence, asking questions, thinking for yourself and excellent decision making) that can prepare children for success in our time.

Children today have so many unique opportunities and at the same time many great challenges. The key is to help them understand the world they are a part of and to prepare them for success in it. It is only through excellent decision making that they can make the most of the opportunities they have rather than wander through life hoping success and happiness finds them. Teach them that they have responsibility for their own development and therefore their future potential depends on hard work and good decision making today.

If you care about the future of your children, commit to use every moment you can spend with them to help them. If you are willing to do this and have a positive attitude, you can give them a chance for greatness and a chance to reach their full potential. If you are up for the challenge of a lifetime – **read on.**

Table of Contents

Step 1 - Choose to Commit to Your Child

Becoming a parent

It's o-dark thirty; your wife is in pain. The doctor seems to be mentally out of the room even when he's here. You and your wife have been building up to this day for months. Somehow it never really seemed real until now. Somehow it seemed like no big deal. People have been having children for many thousands of years. How hard could it really be? Now when it's coming at you at 100 miles an hour it's suddenly terrifying.

You know that your life is about to be changed forever but you just aren't sure what lies ahead. You don't know which path you will be going down, and you don't get to choose. You feel utterly helpless and there is no way to stop it. It's like roller skating down the interstate at night, the wrong way, in a thunderstorm, with razor blades for guardrails.

All at once the baby is out, she cries, the nurse looks her over and then hands her to you – and there you are. All you know is that this little girl needs you – for everything. In this moment, you would give anything, everything, to know that she will be okay. Somehow it does not matter that you have not slept, had hot meal, or had a shower in days. You would do anything for her.

My moment was captured in the cover photo which was taken mere seconds after I set my newborn daughter on the table for the nurse to look her over. Much to my surprise when I spoke to her for the first time, she stopped crying, raised her hand, and grabbed my finger. I knew at this moment that I would do anything for her.

I, like many fathers, had some of my strongest and clearest memories during these moments. For me I was fortunate enough to get to do it four times! Each story was a little different but the outcome is the same. I love each of my children with an intensity that words simply can't express. I am immensely thankful for this as it makes many of the life choices of being a parent easy.

For a brief moment your priorities were simple and clear, so what happened? Why do so many parents allow their priorities to drift away from their children? How could feelings so strong be forgotten? For those willing to make the commitment, parenting can be one of the most rewarding jobs of a lifetime. For many, parenting is an obligation, not a passion. Sadly it seems this is more often the case than not today. Perhaps people are afraid of making a mistake or so worried about being a bad parent that they just can't commit to it.

For those that have children but aren't sure how to be an engaged parent, I ask you to reach back in time and remember your own childhood. Think of those earliest memories that you have. What are the events that stand out the most? Which would you love to do again and which do you wish had never happened? Now it's your turn. You have the time and the opportunity to write your children's history. Make the effort, and teach your children all of the best things you have learned and prepare them for the realities that they face in the future. Give them the love they deserve and the support they won't find anywhere else. Ask yourself, what do you want your children to remember about you?

From the first moment you held your child, you knew your life had changed. Life is now about something much more than just you or your spouse. Engaged parents not only accept these responsibilities, they cherish the opportunity to have them. Being a parent is the best job anyone could ever offer you and the stakes are higher, more permanent, and longer lasting than any six-figure salary could ever be. Being an engaged parent means making the most of your opportunity to prepare your child for success.

Take this moment to make the promise of a lifetime to your children and to yourself. Choose to commit to your children that you will become the living example of what they should strive to live up to in their adult lives. Choose to commit the time and the effort to always be there whenever your children need you. Choose to become a leader for your children and promise to strive for excellence each and every day.

Our Story

Life wasn't always so clear for me or my wife Maya. We met in college and each had dreams of a bright and challenging career. Maya had clear visions of going to medical school and starting her own family practice. I on the other hand was about to finish engineering school and begin my career. During the end of our junior year in college I was helping her prep for the MCAT exams when the inevitable conversation about our future came up. I remember trying to change the subject and even trying to leave but somehow ended up having the dreaded conversation in the stairwell of my friend's apartment building.

I told Maya that she had the rare talent to go to medical school and be successful. I encouraged her to go. I also explained that we had to be realistic about the paths our lives were on and that likely I would not be around when she finished medical school. I knew that I wanted a family, and I could see that would be directly in conflict with her plans. Maya insisted that she could have her own medical practice and still raise a family. I asked her to contact as many doctors as she could find and have an open, honest discussion about balancing the demands of family and the life of a doctor.

Within a few days I left for a job as a summer camp counselor and would be out of reach for the summer. These were the days before e-mail and cell phones, so the only contact I could have with outsiders was good old fashion mail or the payphone just outside the head counselor's office which he seemed to guard twenty-four hours a day. I had a bunk of eleven year old boys that needed constant attention (fourteen of them, actually) and I had never done anything like this before. My goal was simply to have a summer job that was challenging and interesting. I knew that soon I would have more responsibilities and would not be able to take the time to immerse myself into much, outside of my career. I had not planned this to be a fatherhood training experience but its clear now that I learned more about parenting that summer than I had ever intended to.

It was a very big camp with about 400 counselors and about 2000 kids. The summer was soon in full swing and I found myself engrossed in helping the kids. We had to teach them how to make their beds, how to clean the bathroom, and how to put away their clean laundry. The camp did laundry for each cabin only once each week. Many kids only had a few sets of clothes so they had to make their clothes last or be forced to re-wear the cleanest of their dirty clothes.

One evening as we were getting ready to put the kids to bed, the camp leader drove up to my cabin and said I had a phone call. I rode back down to the camp office with him and found that Maya had called him and said she needed to speak with me ASAP. Maya had decided to change her major from pre-med to education so that we could raise a family together. I was stunned, thrilled and immensely guilty feeling all while the head of the summer camp stared at me from only inches away. I think he was actually trying to listen in on our conversation, wondering what kind of news I was getting, and if he was going to need to hire a new counselor. Maya clearly was hoping for a more exited reaction from me than the forced – "that's great" that I gave.

I had to ask Maya if I could call her back so we could talk privately. As we talked out her decision and her plans to tell her parents, I couldn't help but worry that somehow I had manipulated her into changing her whole life around. She assured me that this was not the case, and in fact she thanked me for getting her to take a serious look at her future plans before finishing her undergraduate degree.

As the summer went on we exchanged dozens of letters back and forth. At the end of the summer I left the summer camp a few days early so we could take a weekend away together to talk before school started back up. Within eighteen months we were engaged, and the rest is history.

Understanding

We were married the day after Maya finished her student teaching (she finished on Friday and we were married on Saturday afternoon). We went on a two-week honeymoon that I had planned by myself so she had no idea of where we were going and what we would be doing. She was very frustrated when she asked how to pack and I replied, "Just bring a little of everything." For those of you thinking, I can't believe he did that, I knew my new wife well enough to know that she loved surprises and I knew that our honeymoon would be one of the best opportunities to surprise her. It would be fair to say I understood the way my wife thought and what was important to her.

As time went on I began to see that this "understanding" was a unique and special thing that very few of the couples we knew had ever shared. In fact I now believe, after 20 years of marriage, that this aspect of our relationship is one of the key reasons we have been able to weather the storms that life has thrown at us (both literally and figuratively). During the nearly four years that we dated, we established three simple rules. First, we would not criticize or question each other's statements or actions while around friends or family; rather we would assume each other had a good logical reason for their actions (understanding). We agreed to never allow ourselves to believe the other person had ulterior motives or was trying to manipulate us in some way. Second, we agreed to make time to privately talk through anything that we were uncomfortable about during the day in which it occurred (communication). Finally, we agreed to keep a sense of humor and not to take things too personally when we were just teasing each other. By sticking to these rules of understanding, communication and a sense of humor, we showed each other respect and worked through our differences in private as we developed a singular common perspective. This gave us time to get calibrated into how each other would likely think and feel about a given situation.

So what is "understanding"? Think of it as when you have such a complete knowledge of the way someone thinks that you can accurately anticipate how they would respond to a given situation. Have you ever been separated from someone important in your life while you were in a crowded place like an airport or shopping mall? How did you find them again? If you could anticipate how they would respond accurately – then you could say you that understood them. What about when a person tells you everything is fine but somehow deep inside you, you know what they are saying isn't really the truth? This is what I call understanding. Imagine if you could develop this understanding further and even build your relationship around it. I'm not saying you need to be able to finish each other's sentences, but could you write down the top five most important things in your spouse's life, and be correct? If the answer is yes, then congratulations! If not, then you have an opportunity to improve your relationship and the overall quality of your life. While this will undoubtedly be a great deal of hard work and take a lot of time, there are very few things that will pay you back more than a chance to be in a fully engaged relationship with someone you love.

As the years went by we developed other rules for each other such as never wasting time and energy on worrying. Worry is like internal friction in an engine; it just wastes time, energy, and reduces the life of the engine. You should always focus your energy on solving the problem rather than simply worrying about it. We agreed that problems that could be solved with money were not as big as the problems that no amount of money can solve. Most of all we agreed to dedicate ourselves to working together to solve any issue that challenged either of us. Knowing that you have someone on your side working to help you no matter what comes along is one of the best things you can experience in life. Attitude affects everything in a very large way. When you think about it, most problems are really only as big as you choose to make them. If you focus on solving the issue together instead of worrying, you can work through most of life's challenges together while reinforcing your sense of understanding with each other.

Before we had children, I had a motorcycle. When I first started riding, I took the motorcycle safety foundation class (which I would highly recommend to anyone planning to ride a motorcycle). During the class we performed some very challenging and generally uncomfortably tight turns through a course made of cones at moderate speed. To make the turns properly, you had to develop the confidence to look ahead through the turn instead of looking at the front tire. The teacher kept telling us to trust that "the motorcycle will go where the eyes look." In time, I learned that this was true at all times and was a major factor in motorcycle accidents. Motorcycle drivers get very skilled at identifying road hazards and tend to stare directly at them, and doing this often guides the bike directly into the hazard. I learned the hard way to look at the safe area instead of the hazard, and focus my energy on getting the bike safely around the hazard in this way. So what does this have to do with being a parent? Instead of focusing on the problem, you must focus on the solution. Put all of your energy into working together, communicating with each other, using understanding, and keeping a sense of humor so that your relationship will never crash.

So why did we decide to write a book? We often have people that we have never met before comment about how well behaved our kids are. In fact, this happens so frequently that it's become sort of funny when it happens. We are always very proud to receive this feedback and always congratulate the children, since it is their behavior that is being recognized and appreciated. Usually, we get feedback when we go out to eat, but also when standing in line at the grocery store, or at family events. We often see young couples struggling with their children and letting it change their attitude from positive to negative. Many times we feel like we could help but don't feel like it's our place to walk up to strangers and start offering suggestions. Many of our friends have commented that our suggestions have helped them. All in all we figured that we could only help the people that wanted our help and that most couples would be more open to ideas from a book rather than a critique of a situation.

The structure of the book is laid out in 4 main sections: Choose to Commit to Your Child, Develop Your Family Plan, Live Your Plan, and Never Stop Improving.   In the planning section, the ideas are to build the common ground with your spouse and commit to each other to work together towards a common goal. Next, each of you chooses to commit to your child and begin making decisions that benefit the family as a whole rather than either of you as individuals. Build on this foundation by developing a set of goals and plans for your family. In the Live your Plan section, we discuss ideas and examples of what has worked well for us. In the last section, we discuss how to continuously refine and improve your plan.

So where do you start? You start by setting your life goals together.

Step 2 – Develop your Family Plan

Goal setting

If you are going to commit to your child, wouldn't it be helpful if your spouse would do the same? While you are at it, you need to make sure you and your spouse are committed to each other! The idea here is that life is hard and it takes work. You have a much better chance for success and happiness if the two of you can work together towards the same things. Marriages that last have both spouses committed to achieving the same goals and a commitment to work with each other to do it. They promise to support each other in pursuit of these common goals. If you and your spouse don't have the same goals it's going to be very hard to achieve anything.

One way to get started is to make a list of people you admire, and why you feel this way. Once each of you completes this list, share your list with your spouse and talk about it. When you have some things you both agree are important, determine which of these things you currently do well and which you don't. Begin converting the list of things you don't currently do well into goals for each other (both things to work on together and individually). What are the things other people see in you? If you don't know – ask. Just be careful to only ask for feedback on the specific things for which you are willing to accept criticism. Don't ask for feedback if you aren't willing to change.

By asking someone to give you open and honest feedback you are asking that person to take a risk. He or she might say something that will make you mad or that will change your feelings towards them. If they trust you not to bite their head off, they will likely give you some very useful information that could help you achieve your goals. Don't expect honest feedback unless you can sit respectfully and listen (not just hear – but truly listen and understand) to everything the person has to say. Thank them for their help; don't interrogate them. It's okay to come back later with two or three carefully worded questions, but don't push it too far or the person will tell you whatever you want to hear so that you will just go away.

Now make a list of things that are most important to you in life and have your spouse do the same. Compare lists, talk about them, and make a new consolidated list that contains only the things you both can agree about. Now take these lists and work together on one new list that is intended to tell your child how to live a successful life. Try to get at least ten fundamental elements that you both agree are important and would be helpful to your child. I call this list the Keys to a Successful Life. The list my wife and I created is in the appendix for your reference – but don't look at it before you come up with a first draft of your own list. Our ideas are simply that – ours; they may not align with your goals. The point here is to get you to think about what is important to you and make sure you and your spouse agree so you can jointly make decisions that support your goals. I challenge you to think for yourself and I encourage you to teach your kids to do the same.

The lists described above, plus your Keys to a Successful Life, are the beginning of what I call The Family Plan.

The Family Plan

How do you make a family plan? You need to begin with the perspective that family comes first. Constructing a family plan is hard work and will require time with your spouse to work through the key facts together. Your life has many elements to it, and each of these elements needs to fit together like pieces of a puzzle. The idea is to sit down and work through each of these elements together with your spouse. Once the family plan is written you will have a common set of goals to work towards as a family. Each member will have a role to play and a set of responsibilities to contribute towards making these goals into a reality. Each element of this plan is covered under a separate section of this book to provide sufficient details and examples of how to get your plan together. Keep in mind that there is no one way to do this, no right or wrong answers, there is only your family's way. The examples presented should be considered conversation starters only. I will present only *a way* to write a family plan, not *the way*. Our family plan has five books: Protect; Provide; Prepare for Success; Happy, Healthy, and Fulfilled; Emergency.

Parents' responsibilities are summarized as the three P's. You need to Protect your children, Provide for your children and Prepare your children for success. The details of how you will fulfill each of these responsibilities come together as a comprehensive set of parenting goals. You will also need to consider your long term personal goals outside of your parenting goals. I call these the things that will help you become happy, healthy and fulfilled.

Your family plan may have a different structure. It may consist of more sections, or less. Pulling together this plan will take time and hard work, but most of all it takes working together with your spouse. Only by working together can you truly commit to make your dreams into reality. Once these elements of your family plan are on paper you have a beginning – not an end. You could and should change it as you think and talk more about it in the future. Be sure not to change something significant in your plan unless you and your spouse discuss it and agree. Remember this is a family plan, not a list of personal wants.

Protect

Protecting your children is instinctive and seems natural. The key here is to develop and agree on how to achieve this goal together. When you think of protecting your children you may think of things like teaching them not to talk to strangers, and washing their hands before eating. These are, of course, good ideas. However, the only way to truly protect your children is teach them to think for themselves. They must learn to seek out information, ask questions, and be skeptical of the information they get. Teach them never to be fearful but instead to understand life's hazards and minimize risk by making good decisions and always being prepared.

Good decision making is one of the greatest defining factors that separate people that are successful from those that are not. Given good information and sufficient time to consider the facts logically, anyone can be a good decision maker. In order to teach your kids to think for themselves, you will first need to develop this skill for yourself. If you aren't sure what I mean, think about the movie <u>The Runaway Bride</u>, in which she is struggling to figure out which kind of eggs she actually likes. She found out that for her entire life she had simply gone with what her boyfriend at the time liked, but never actually thought about it for herself. She had to start over from the beginning and try several different ways to eat eggs to figure out what she preferred. This process is exactly what I'm trying to explain. Thinking for yourself is hard work and time consuming, but it's the most empowering thing you can do for yourself and your children.

Learning to think for yourself and being prepared takes practice, so this is one reason I like taking my kids camping. I take the older kids backpacking where the need for well thought out preparation is much greater. As parents it can be very hard to let your kids fail and learn something the hard way. Camping provides many opportunities for kids to understand the consequences of their mistakes quickly. Kids learn a great deal from small mistakes such as leaving a bag of chips out too long and finding that the squirrels have eaten them. Teach your kids what to do and explain why it is important, and then follow-up to make sure they do what they need to do. I tell my wife, "You need to inspect what you expect or don't expect anything at all." Sometimes you have to allow your kids to make mistakes and suffer the consequences to be sure they really understand and commit to thinking things through on their own next time.

In order to teach your kids to be well prepared, you need to develop your own everyday preparations and let them understand why your plan makes sense. Encourage your kids to ask questions and even offer suggestions for your plans. Key elements of our plan include simple things like having first aid kits in each of our cars, being aware of our surroundings, learning self-defense techniques, and developing a home defense plan.

We also have elements for how we plan to teach our kids how to protect themselves. Three of them currently study martial arts. Most of all we refer them back to our Keys to a Successful Life document. They would tell you that gathering their own information and thinking for themselves are the most important ways to protect themselves. We teach them to be aware of their surroundings, and also to protect each other and stick up for each other. Along with this, we have some simple phrases we teach the kids such as: "Stupid hurts", "dares are for dummies", and "if you are going to pull the tiger's tail, then you better have a plan for his teeth."

The key aspect of protecting the kids is teaching them to understand that life is about taking calculated risks. Before you try something new you need to gather information to help you understand the risks. Then you need to think about how to reduce the risk by looking at the elements of risk separately (likelihood, severity, and frequency). Once this is understood, then develop plans to reduce each of these elements independently.

During the years I rode a motorcycle, I made mental notes about motorcycle wrecks of which I heard. Usually I found that several risks had been elevated at the same time such as the driver being overtired, driving in the dark, driving in heavy traffic, and driving in the rain. I decided to manage each of these risks separately by planning do my motorcycle riding early in the day, when rain was not in the forecast, on back roads away from heavy traffic. While I had events and circumstances where I decided to drive at night, in the rain, or in heavy traffic, I never had the combination of these things. In this way I enjoyed riding a motorcycle with a lower level of risk due to my preparations.

Another example would be when we recently had a vacation at the beach. Maya took the kids swimming in the ocean and she got stung by a jellyfish. The kids were upset but we explained that it was a risk that we knew about and had accepted (since it was unlikely and of a low severity). We also knew what to do and handled the situation calmly due to our preparations. These situations and the resulting experiences reinforce that it's much better to be prepared, take calculated risks, and live a rich and full life, rather than to be fearful.

Provide

In some ways providing is one thing that American families seem to be almost obsessed with. Parents often shower their kids with more possessions than the kids ever imagined or even wanted. The results tend to foster kids with little appreciation for the value of a dollar and short attention spans. Teach your kids to be grateful for what they have, treat all items (not matter what you paid for them) with respect, and donate items generously to others that need them if your children lose interest.

The type of providing I intend to discuss here goes much deeper than things your children can get from the store. You need to provide them with love, support, and a sense of belonging. Show them an unlimited commitment to always be there for them. Teach them that you will always love and support them no matter what. This foundation will help them develop self-confidence and a willingness to try new things. You need to provide them with a little bit of bedrock to lean on when they need it.

No matter how many or how few possessions kids have, it's the small things that matter the most. In the long term, kids value things they associate with positive memories and influential people more than the latest video game. Focus on providing your time and energy above your money and you will always be on the right track. With four children, it is difficult to get one-on-one time with each child. One time my wife took our third child out on errands, and left the rest of the kids at home with me. When they were finished, they went through the McDonald's drive through and got a Sprite. Years later, my daughter still talks about that time with Mommy. Something as insignificant as errands and a Sprite can make a lasting positive memory.

Many times my kids enjoy making things from cardboard boxes and scraps of paper just as much as playing with the toys they get from the store. When it comes time to spend money, look for items that will last and be useful for a very long time. I still have many of the toys I played with as a kid: Match Box cars, Legos, Lincoln Logs, Erector Sets, army trucks, marbles, dominos, and books. If your kids treat their toys with respect they may be able to share their toys with their own kids as I have done. The added benefit of passing on your toys to your children is to further deepen the connection with them. You should capitalize on every opportunity to discuss what you remember from growing up and have them tell you about the similarities and differences they can see. You need to recall as much as possible about the key moments in your life and try to pass on these lessons to your kids.

Look for new experiences you can provide for your kids like playing sports, going to the zoo, playing the piano, target shooting, or going to a musical. Most of all spend time together outdoors. Our kids love going camping, taking hikes, and catching critters of all types. These are the experiences that will last. We teach them practical skills like how to build a camp fire and how to cook a freshly caught fish over the fire. These skills build self-confidence and help them build an identity that is unique from many of their peers. They are very proud to tell their friends of their adventures and whenever possible, they enjoy teaching their friends their new found skills.

Our plan for providing for our kids also includes elements for our financial plan: Saving for retirement, saving for our kids' education, and our monthly budget. These plans keep us on track with our annual goals. Our annual goals are set to provide a balance of saving for the near term needs like vacations and Christmas presents, and longer term goals of saving to buy a car, the kids' college education, and our own retirement. There are lots of books written about financial planning so I do not need to go into this any further here. The concept is for you and your spouse to lay out a plan together that supports your family plan goals and then work together to achieve your goals. Remember to make time to acknowledge annual milestones and celebrate the success you achieve. When you find some elements that didn't go according to plan, discuss them openly and agree on some changes that will work better for the family as a whole.

Prepare for Success

Put simply, success comes from grit. Our founding fathers had grit; they had to in order to survive the many challenges they faced. Imagine how our country would have been different if our founding fathers had given up. Imagine how the world would be different today without the many heroes our country has been blessed with. Grit is an element of character that is admired and respected universally around the world. Why is that? It is because grit is the one common element to all those heroes in the world. You need grit to be successful. Show your children your grit and teach them to have grit as well.

Grit is about standing up to adversity, believing in yourself, and never giving up. In many ways you define yourself by how you deal with failure. Those that rise up after failure and learn to try harder next time will ultimately succeed in the long run. Organized sports can provide opportunities to develop grit if the coaches have a good character and the right perspective of what is important. It is always important to be involved with your kids to discuss their experiences (whether good or bad). Encourage your kids to challenge themselves to try new things and not to be afraid of failure because this is how we learn.

On our most recent camping trip, our seven year old daughter tried at least twenty times over the course of the trip to get up on water skis. She was cold, her hands kept slipping, and she got water in her face and up her nose. So why did she keep trying over and over again? Because she has grit! You can probably imagine how proud she was when she was finally successful. Take a moment and consider how significant this success was for our daughter and how much this is likely to influence her future behavior then next time she faces adversity. Providing the opportunity for her to challenge herself and being there to offer encouragement is what engaged parents do to help their kids learn to believe in themselves.

We recently took our oldest two kids snow skiing for the first time, and spent lots of time on the ground as a result. The key is to never give up and always have a positive attitude, and a sense of humor. When our kids fell, we would help them think about what may have caused the fall, and how to prevent it next time. We also kept plenty of M&M's and Jolly Ranchers in our pockets to help keep spirits high.

Talking to your kids is the key.   Your kids will learn what is important to you if you talk to them about it. We take advantage of discussions with the kids to emphasize the following concepts and others from our Keys to a Successful Life:

Is better to try and fail than to never try at all.

Whether you believe you can or believe you can't – you are right. Attitude is everything.

Use your time wisely and take advantage of opportunities that come your way.

We are like most people, in that we are constantly busy doing our jobs and going about the daily routines at home. We have precious little free time and how we use it is very telling about what is important to us. Make sure that you think about how you use your free time and be sure it is meaningful. How you spend your free time is, in many ways, is what defines you as a person and what your kids will remember about you. Teach your kids to use their free time wisely and this will set them up for lifetime of discovery and achievement instead of dismal "me time" filled with video games and mindless TV.

What makes you different is what you are passionate about. Tell your children what you are passionate about and why. Live your life in a way that people can tell what you are passionate about. It's always useful to ask your friends what they see in you and how you live your life. Help your children explore the world and discover their passion, and then spend your free time with them being passionate about being a good parent.

As your children learn what is most important to them, and learn how to use their time wisely, you can add in another element – teach them to take advantage of opportunities that come their way.

Education Plan

The largest and most detailed part of our Prepare for Success plan is our Education Plan. If you have read this far into the book it likely comes as no surprise that my wife and I decided to homeschool our kids. It is safe to say that this has been one of the best decisions that we have made since getting married. As of the writing of this book, our oldest two children have participated in state standardized testing and have scored far above grade level.

You might think that with scores like these we must not ever have time for fun and yet we take more family vacations and fun trips out of town than anyone we know. Since the kids are flexible with their schedules we make a point to take days off from time to time to go to the zoo, the science center, the theater, or the beach. My oldest son finished his second baseball season and his team won the championship for the last two years in a row. My oldest daughter enjoys tending to her collection of pets that ranges from frogs, to caterpillars, and many others in between. She recently won first place in her division at the regional science fair for a project she completed on aquaponics.

The decision to homeschool our children was for us a liberating and empowering choice. As you can imagine we spent a great deal of time discussing the choice of my wife leaving her career as a private school science teacher to start her career as stay-at-home mom and homeschool teacher. Together we wrote a list of Why We Choose to Home School which we have included in the appendix.

My grandmother was a teacher in a one-room schoolhouse. She often said that it was the most effective form of education there was. She noticed the older kids paying attention to some of the younger kids' lessons for subjects in which they struggled but didn't want to admit they needed help. Being in the same room gave them a chance for remedial lessons without the guilt or embarrassment. She also noticed that the younger kids often listened to lessons intended for the older kids. The younger kids may not have understood everything but they had a good understanding of what they would be learning in the future. They also gained a greater understanding for why it was important to thoroughly learn the basic skills. They were able to see the big picture of the entire twelve years of their education, which gave them a good perspective and a great opportunity to learn how and why learning was so important.

Once we decided to homeschool our children, we had to develop a plan of how to do it. In order to do this well we needed great examples, so we did some research. We decided we would draw from example education plans from public schools in our state, as well as education plans from several states that had the best standardized test scores. We also looked at examples of a solid private school plans, public school education plans, other homeschooling plans, and education plans from what were considered to be some of the best international public education systems in the world such as Singapore.

The process we used to compare these education plans is known as "benchmarking". There are many books and on-line articles available on this subject so there is no need to describe this in detail here. The idea is to take an organized approach and glean the key facts that help you compare and contrast your ideas and the ideas of others. Once the comparison process is finished, then you must develop your process to fill in the gaps in your education plan. Even if you are not currently planning to homeschool, you still should go through the process of benchmarking to be sure the education you have chosen for your child measures up. Don't believe that the education of your children is anyone's responsibility other than your own. You have committed to prepare your child for success. Make sure you are at the very least aware of, if not engaged in everything your kids are doing at school. Remember that public school is only one of many options and it will need to be supplemented in certain areas.

Incorporate the elements from your Keys to a Successful Life into your education plan. Make sure that your education plan covers all of the elements that you think are important and have helped you achieve success in your life. Then figure out the best way to teach the concepts. Be open to doing things outside of the classroom environment. Take time to do experiment, take trips, and have discussions. Remember, you are teaching skills that will last a lifetime. Take the time to do it right. If you spent time developing a list of things that are important to you or your spouse, take time to discuss what ideas you could add into your education plan to make it better.

This process is important regardless of how you plan to educate your children. Always remember, your kids are counting on you to help prepare them for success. If you choose to use the public education system, you must get involved with what they are learning and make a point to discuss their school day with them – everyday. You need to discuss what they learned today to help address questions, to give your perspective and to show them that their education is so important to you that you intend to check in with them every day. While you may feel you do not have time for this, you will be amazed at how much you can do in just fifteen minutes each day if you fully focus your attention on interacting with your child. If you have trouble finding fifteen minutes each day for your children, you may need to look harder at your daily schedule and ask yourself what your kids would say about what seems to be most important to you.

This daily interaction is critical to do whether homeschooling, attending private school, or public school. Your background and experience will be very helpful to your kids as they work through their daily challenges. It is incredibly important to have this interaction with your kids. It is only this way that you can determine if your children's education process is working up to the standards and expectations you had planned. If you and your spouse determine that the public or private school you have chosen does not fulfill your educational goals for your child, then you need to search for an educational solution that fulfills those goals.

Make sure to document the education history of each of your children. This is to ensure you covered every element in your plan and also to use for future school year planning. Also document any significant conversations. If you take time to talk to your kids about a subject, it's worth documenting.

Emergency Plan

Our Emergency Plan is pretty much what you would expect it to be. We live in an area that is subject to hurricanes so we have a section on hurricane preparedness. We have an evacuation checklist so we don't need to think about what to do if the time comes when we need to evacuate. Our evacuation plan is very specific and gives step by step instructions of who will do what. It explains what to get from where and where to put it. The idea is to give step by step instructions for the entire family so that we can get the work done in the most efficient way possible without having to remember much of anything.

We have a list of valuables: What the item is, and where it is located. If we have extra time and extra room in our vehicle, we can easily grab some of our valuables.

If we decide that staying home is a better option than evacuating, we have an inventory of extra food and water. The foods that we inventory are things that we normally eat on a weekly basis, so we regularly rotate our food storage to avoid keeping out of date items on the shelf. We also have an extensive medical kit (more than just a basic first aid kit) that we keep in a bucket, so we can easily transport it if necessary.

We also have a tornado plan, medical emergency plan and home defense plan (also part of our protect plan).

Documents that are a part of our Emergency plan include the following:

Contact list- names, addresses, and phone numbers of family members and friends

Medical history- a detailed history of every illness, doctor's appointment, and surgeries for each family member

Kid's notes- when the kids do something cute or memorable, we write it down and keep it in a notebook

Happy, Healthy & Fulfilled

The goal is to understand what you need and what you want out of life and then write it down on paper so you and your spouse can work together to make it happen. If you don't know what you want out of life then you and your spouse have lots to talk about. Better to get it out in the open sooner rather than later! Whatever you decide is up to you, but the first step to making it happen is to talk about it.

This plan is primarily focused on my wife and me, and the things we identified that are important us, other than those things that are already covered in the other four plans. Imagine on your 100th birthday you were asked to tell the story of your life. What would you want to describe? To us, we wanted to be happy, healthy and fulfilled on our 100th birthdays. What do you wish for?

Think about the things that you want to be remembered for and make sure you project those things everyday of your life. A good test is to ask people who know you well to describe what things they think are most important to you. If what these people describe matches closely to your "what is most important to me" list than you are doing well at projecting what is important to you. If there are gaps, then this feedback gives you a chance to make some adjustments. Make sure you take any feedback you receive with an open mind and thank those that care enough to be honest with you. Be careful not to damage your relationships by challenging why they offered the feedback they did or else you will never get honest feedback again.

What does it mean to be happy and how do your build your life so that you can be happy a lot of the time? I offer this quote from a local church for consideration – "Happiness is not getting what you want, but wanting what you get." When you consider the full scope of what life can throw at you, surely you can see how wanting to have all of the things that you have could be a good definition for happiness. The key here is that few of us would choose to look at our lives from this perspective. Many people choose to focus on the things they wanted but didn't get with so much energy and emotion that they prevent themselves from being appreciative for the good things they do have. Take time each day to count your blessings with your children and show them how to be grateful for the life that they have.

One of the best explanations I have seen for happiness involved a pyramid diagram that displays the essential needs for life including food and shelter as layers stacked on top of one another in priority order. Only when the lower layers are satisfied can an individual shift focus to the next level or higher order needs. Each additional layer is another step forward in improving your overall quality of life. For more on this concept do an internet search on the phrase "hierarchy of needs".

This model makes it easy to see how our focus shifts whenever more fundamental needs are threatened. Turning this concept upside down you can see that in order to spend time developing and practicing things at the higher levels you most have a strong foundation in place. This is the fundamental concept in the idea behind developing your family plan. Once the entire family is engaged and committed to achieving the goals outlined in your plan, you have a strong foundation in place. With the family plan in full effect, you can now ascend to new levels of fulfillment in your life. Now that you have the chance to be more fulfilled, what action will you take? It's time for more planning.

As you have experiences in life, the more significant moments (the good and the bad) tend to stay clear in your memory. The more subtle events tend to fade. It is critically important to document your life to recall these moments. As you reflect on past experiences your sense of fulfillment comes from the satisfaction that you have lived your life in a way that you wanted to and are proud of. Be sure to document the things you are most proud of so that you can teach others about what you did and why it is so important to you. Also, you can enjoy reflecting on your achievements if you have them well documented. Fulfillment is a backward looking emotion; it's in the past. You can't experience fulfillment about a meal that you have not eaten, but you can experience fulfillment for having prepared it for your family. Happiness is in the immediate term; it's in the here and now and can come and go in an instant. Fulfillment, once achieved, is long term and everlasting regardless of any future events.

Fulfillment can be experienced over and over again for the same event, kind of like watching a re-run on TV. Documenting key experiences in your life can increase the happiness in your life by allowing you to re-live pleasant moments again and again, so why not document as many of these moments as possible? You can experience happiness and fulfillment at the same time in this way if you are reflecting on a happy moment that you worked hard to achieve.

The key to being happy and fulfilled at the same time is to challenge yourself to be the best and most the you can be (richness of character) and to spend time doing the actions that fulfill you the most (richness of life). You must identify the character attributes that you admire in others and then commit yourself to develop these within yourself. Then you must spend your time doing what fulfills you.

To try to explain fulfillment, you need to think of it as a thing with many separate parts that together add up together to create the experience of being fulfilled (similar to ingredients for a fine meal). Each of these parts contributes a small amount to the overall experience. Any event in your life can provide fulfillment in multiple ways at the same time.

Certainly fulfillment is a complex and emotional thing with elements that are tied to how difficult or unlikely a positive outcome is expected to be. The difficulty aspect is a very personally emotional matter in terms of the context of the challenge. People often have areas where they feel extremely comfortable but usually have just as many areas where they feel extremely uncomfortable. Working together with your spouse you can help each other to overcome fears, benefit from past experiences and increase each other's level of fulfillment.

Fulfillment occurs at different levels of intensity based on the circumstances. For example, you may be satisfied after hosting a successful family event but you would likely experience a much more intense level of satisfaction if the significance of the event were greater. To take this to an extreme example, imagine the satisfaction you may experience from winning a marathon or climbing Mount Everest. The key point here is that fulfillment is linked strongly to emotions. The greater the intensity of the associated emotions, the greater the intensity of satisfaction or sense of failure. To live your life to the fullest, you have to be willing to take some calculated risks.

As we tell our kids, you should never worry as this is just wasted energy. Instead, understand the risks and be prepared for them. The best way to be prepared is to become expert planners. You need to plan for what you hope occurs and also for all reasonable potential outcomes. Preparation starts with research to understand what could go wrong and what your back-up plan will be if this occurs. You can often learn a great deal from websites but it is always best to speak with people who have first-hand experience.

We recently took the kids on a whitewater kayaking trip, and while my wife and I have extensive whitewater rafting experience, neither of us had ever kayaked before. Fortunately, we also have canoe experience. We spoke with a guide service and they answered our questions. After the telephone conversation with the guide, we felt we had what we needed to have a great experience and do it safely. It turned out we were over prepared (as we usually are) but we had a great experience and our kids can't wait to go back and do it again.

Experience is the very best way to learn what to expect and how to handle adversity. In order to gain experience, you must challenge yourself to try new things, and then go out and do them. Plan to try new things (plan & prepare to minimize risk) – then do it and learn from your mistakes – then do it again. Each time you do this, you learn more and get better. What we have discovered is that you can often leverage what you learn from one set of experiences and apply it to unrelated areas for other future adventures (such as water skiing and snow skiing or camping and emergency planning).

Sharing your experiences with others

One of the things I enjoy most is to share my knowledge and experience with others. I enjoy both the opportunity to teach and the chance to re-live my experience through story telling. As this is one of my most fulfilling experiences, I have spent a lot of time thinking about how to do more of it and how to do a better job each time. To understand this concept further consider what people are interested in, to what extent they are interested and how intense of an experience they desire or are expecting.

Most people would think of climbing Mount Everest to be the challenge of a lifetime. For those that choose to do this and are successful, they experience a tremendous level of pride and satisfaction in their experience that provides them with fulfillment. Some of their satisfaction comes from telling other people (people who are interested in mountain climbing) about their journey. But what if the people they are speaking to could care less about mountain climbing? Does this change the fulfillment experience? Certainly a person who selected climbing Mount Everest as their lifetime goal and then achieved it would always have fulfillment in having achieved this goal. Some amount of fulfillment is gained by re-living the experience while telling the story. This component of fulfillment may not be as good if the experiences are unlikely for other people to appreciate if they can't relate to it or understand why it was important to you.

Fulfillment comes from many distinctly different aspects of your life. You can feel good about achieving a goal you set for yourself or feel satisfied about helping someone in need. You can also re-live these moments over and over when describing your actions to someone for the first time.

The goal in understanding fulfillment further is to help understand and therefore plan future events in your life that are most likely to give you the maximum amount of fulfillment. Think of fulfillment as a combination of factors such as:

Sense of achievement

Friend or family member bond building

Enjoyment derived from the opportunity to tell your story to others

Negative consequences

It would be impossible to calculate the net value in any quantitative way but in a qualitative sense you could imagine adding and subtracting some measure of value for each of these factors and finding some form of net satisfaction from any given event. The idea would be to understand what things give you the highest overall satisfaction and then focus your time doing those things.

So how do we use this information to improve our quality of life? The goal should be to use your free time in ways that help provide you with more fulfilling events. To understand one way you could do this, try this exercise. Begin by reflecting on happy moments in your life and stories about your past you are proud of or enjoy telling people about. Next, make a list of the things that you enjoy doing or that help to describe things you are proud of about yourself. This list is starting to paint a picture that describes what you are doing when you are happy or what you have achieved when you are fulfilled.

Sort these things into groups and create a very simplified list of these activities – let's call this list your level one list. Now look at each item in your level one list and describe in as must detail as possible the context in which these activities occur. Each of these new lists are your level two lists. Review each of these level two lists to see where you can add further detail and explanation. Try to think about your interests and answer the questions (how much, how often, and to what extent). As you look at what you have just created, keep in mind that you are trying to develop a greater understanding of what makes you happy or allows you to feel fulfilled. The description you have created is only a beginning and will need to be updated as you gain new experiences or recall other things that need to be added.

The items that you have described most completely are the things that you are most passionate about. Focus first on these, and then to a lesser extend focus on the other items. With these items in mind, begin to plan what an ideal week of everyday life, (not vacation) should look like if you could have more time for activities that make you happy. It's very important to create a realistic and achievable plan. Then consider the activities that need to be reserved for more specific circumstances or time of the year. Describe these as fully as possible with every detail of context from your lists. Next, develop a list of activities for annual vacations. Finally, describe things that you would like to do once every several years or simply one time things.

What you have created is a planning guide of the things that you would like to see yourself doing with details, circumstances and time frame. Keep in mind that this exercise was a very simplified look at what ideas you have to improve the quality of your life and the richness of your life. The value and usefulness of what you create will be in direct proportion the time and effort you put into the project. If done well, this document, alongside your spouses', could help you work together to achieve a richer and more satisfying quality of life today and in the future.

If you repeat this exercise with your older, more mature children, this process may help you plan more satisfying experiences for the future such as family vacations or even be the beginings for a retirement plan.

A final concept to consider is that the full richness of life includes both positive and negative experiences. I once heard enjoyment of camping described as the satisfaction of mutual suffering. There is certainly truth to the idea that overcoming difficult or unpleasant experiences together is yet another way to experience fulfillment. While no one would intentionally plan to have negative experiences, when they do occur keep a positive attitude and make the most of them. My wife and I have several situations that most would classify as negative yet we look back on most of them very fondly.

During one experience, we were traveling by car in a very intense snow storm. We had a front wheel drive car with chains on and had been driving all day. When the windshield wipers froze up and stopped clearing away the snow, I pulled over and replaced the windshield wiper blades (luckily I was prepared with a spare set). When these froze up, I put my skiing goggles on and stuck my head out the window. When we finally realized we couldn't get home that night we started looking for a hotel. When we saw a hotel on a hill with lights on, we pulled off the highway with plans of staying there. We had been traveling in just a few inches of snow on the highway behind a plow truck and didn't realize that the exit ramp was covered with over a foot of deep snow. Luckily there was a closed gas station at the bottom of the ramp, so we gunned the engine to keep us moving and get off the highway ramp. We felt a tremendous sense of achievement when we safely reached the gas station – now all we had to do was go in the hotel and get some rest.

The snow was so deep we couldn't even see where the street was located. As we looked up the hill at the hotel, we saw the road was unplowed and the driveway was extremely steep. We considered trying to get back on the highway but realized this wasn't feasible. We walked over to where we thought the entrance to the hotel likely was and started kicking around in the snow looking for the break in the concrete curb. After nearly an hour of looking, we had scouted the hotel street and marked the edges with red plastic drink cups we just happened to have with us. We said a little prayer and decided that it was now or never. Somehow we managed to make it up the hill only to be told the hotel was sold out! I had Maya gather our plastic cups while I spoke with the manager about our options.

After several minutes of discussion, the manager admitted that he did have a honeymoon suite with a hot tub available but it was very expensive. I took the room and surprised Maya. We spent most of the night soaking in a heart shaped hot tub, eating pizza, watching a Cop's marathon on TV and occasionally looking out the window to see the snow continue to pile deeper and deeper. We called our family to let them know we were not only okay, but having fun. Our families had been so worried and remarked about how odd it seemed to them that we were actually enjoying the trip. After a long a stressful day, most people would be grumpy, yet we chose to have a positive attitude and be grateful for a warm place to rest.

Sometimes a movie or TV show will introduce an idea that makes me think, often for several days, about an idea. In an episode of "Star Trek – The Next Generation" the captain was given a chance to go back in time and change one element of his past and see how his life would be different. The episode was called "Tapestry" and portrayed the concept that a person's life was like a tapestry. The analogy was that changing one element of your past was equivalent to pulling a thread of the tapestry which inevitably causes the entire thing to come undone. The captain ended up regretting the change to his life far more than living with his past. In the end he was able to restore his life to the way it had originally occurred. The key here was that he was now grateful and appreciative of what he had, instead of regretful about his past. Most people would benefit from this mindset shift if they could only see things this way.

Step 3 - Live Your Plan – Everyday

Our First Day at Home as New Parents

No matter how you look at it, the first day at home with the new baby (especially your first) is a day you will never forget. For me, it was almost as negative as positive. My wife and I had a big fight in the dining room in front of the entire family just as dinner was being served. It was definitely not one of my proudest moments but it all worked out for the best in the end.

We had failed to talk about or plan for our new life with the baby with any level of detail before going to the hospital. My wife had read many books on pregnancy and delivery, and almost nothing about how to take care of a baby. When we came home after six days of stress and general lack of sleep we found out that was a big mistake. When it was time to have dinner (my first real meal in days) the baby began to cry, and my wife began to get up from the dinner table to respond. I flat out insisted that my wife sit down and eat with the family while I attended to the baby. After approximately ten minutes of her crying I decided that it was was going to take a while to settle her down. I set my new baby carefully into her crib and gently closed the bedroom door. When I arrived at the table to have some dinner, my wife sprang up like she was launched from an ejection seat. When I asked her to sit down and finish her dinner, the fireworks started.

After a few emotional weeks we went to the doctor for our daughter's six week check-up. Everything was good except we were having trouble adjusting to the nearly twenty-four hour a day neediness of our new daughter. The doctor gave us a feeding schedule to try. Within a day or two we learned that if we could stall the baby for three hours in between feedings, she was able to get much more milk, be more satisfied, and sleep longer. We found that if we stuck to a routine life got a whole lot better. By feeding nearly constantly my wife had almost nothing to give the baby and the baby was never truly satisfied. The emotional stress of putting the baby down and letting her cry was too much for my post partum wife to handle, at least at first. Once we got into a routine, we all caught up on our sleep, had a few good meals, and began really enjoying every moment we had together.

While it sounds harsh, we found that if we knew that the baby was safe, well fed, not too hot or too cold, and had a clean diaper, but still insisted on crying, we should give her the opportunity to calm herself in her bed. The first three nights of this sleep training, she cried for over an hour the first night, about forty-five minutes the second night, and only fifteen minutes the third night. We never let her cry for more than ten minutes at a time without checking on her. We would go into her room and check on her to make sure she didn't have any reasons to cry, (dirty diaper, something pinching her, etc.) Then we would put her back in her bed and reset the timer. After the third night, she had trained herself how to fall asleep on her own, and from then on very rarely cried when we would put her down to sleep in her crib.

This lesson has been one we have shared with literally dozens of new parents. Very few couples are able to handle the emotional stress of adjusting to the routine and sometimes having to let your baby cry. The parents that did establish the feeding and sleeping routine were pleased with the outcome.

Some input from Maya- As you can imagine, asking a brand new, post-partum mother to ignore her new baby's crying created some tension between Keith and me. I realized in those first few days of being a new mother that I should have focused less on reading about pregnancy and childbirth, and more on what to do once we arrived home with the baby! There were many books that we read as new parents, but a few stand out as extremely helpful. The <u>On Becoming Babywise</u> series by Garry Ezzo and Robert Bucknam was essential in learning how to establish a routine and how to change the routine at different stages of the baby's life. <u>Secrets of the Baby Whisperer</u> by Tracy Hogg taught us to understand what our baby was communicating, and was also helpful in understanding what the baby needed in her daily schedule.

Communication

Learning from others requires communication, which takes effort by both parties. One person crafts a deliberate message and the other person pays attention, listens, and then interprets the message. Communication and learning are so important to human survival that both sides of this process are instinctual. Both teaching and listening take effort and while the desire to participate in this process is instinctual, being skilled in teaching and in learning is most definitely something that has to be developed, refined, and practiced.

New born children may not yet have the ability to express themselves using words. However, they communicate very effectively with their parents through a series of different types of crying and body language. There are several books written on the subject of interpreting messages babies are sending which are very helpful. In addition, there are several books that instruct parents on how to teach their infant children a simple sign language to make this communication much easier to understand.

Working to teach your baby is an extremely positive way to interact with them. Helping them communicate greatly reduces the need for crying as the primary form of communication and self-reinforces the value in effective communication for both parties. When the child is able to ask for something and receives it in a timely manner a series of good things begin to happen. Brain development is accelerated, the desire to expand the communication by both parent and child helps to grow the attention span of the child, and the positive attention helps both parent and child turn otherwise frustrating moments into positive learning moments.

We began to teach baby sign language within the first 3 months of age and effective communication took place by the time the baby developed motor skills enough to perform the motions (around 6 months old). We chose to teach a few signs that were important at that age- "more please", "all done", "hungry", and "thirsty" were the signs we focused on.

Part of the learning process also includes speaking to your child as you would another adult (in terms of language). Make sure to speak clearly and slowly and explain concepts and reasons why you take certain actions. Your child has much more understanding capability than you could possibly imagine. If you speak to him and help him learn without silly baby speak, you will soon be amazed by what he has to say to you. As your child begins to talk, teach him to ask for things by talking or signing, instead of fussing and whining. Expect your child to speak to you and others politely. Teach him to ask for things nicely, and to answer you respectfully when you ask him to do something. Be clear and consistent in your expectations for communication with your child.

Another way you can teach your baby how to communicate is by reading to him every day, starting in infancy. My wife began reading to each of our children when she was nursing. She would read out loud whatever she happened to be reading at the time- a newspaper article, a book about parenting, or a science magazine. We both would read children's books to the kids, talking about colors, shapes, names of objects, and animal sounds. We would count things in books, and talk about rhyming words and opposites. As they got older we would ask the kids to predict what they thought would happen next, and discuss why the character chose to do a certain thing, or what our children would do if they were in that situation.

Practice your active listening skills when your kids are speaking to you. Make sure to show them the same respect that you expect in return when you are speaking. Ask them clarifying questions to show that you are listening to them. When you have something else that is demanding your attention, explain that to them and even get them involved in what you are working on whenever possible. Finally, make sure to develop true understanding between you and your children. The goal should be that they can accurately predict what you would say to them in any given situation.

Build credibility with your kids by saying what you mean and meaning everything you say. It's impossible to un-say something once spoken so make sure to always set a good example for your children. Remember the old saying, "If you can't say something nice, don't say anything at all." Kids will remember everything you say and repeat it at the most embarrassing times, so make sure you think before you speak. Keep your promises and always do what you say you will do. Your children see you and your behavior as the example of what they should do.

Teach kids how to earn your trust, and then give them a chance to earn it. Help them understand the expectations and then coach them on the gaps between your expectations and their actions. Discuss the reasons why something is important. Teach them it's not just some silly rule that you made up; there are good reasons why something is important. When you say no to something, explain why. Sometimes you won't be able to explain in the moment of saying no, but do go back later and explain. This way, your children will learn why you make certain decisions, and hopefully they will learn good decision making for themselves.

Some great examples, written by my wife, Maya

One time I was cooking breakfast while my youngest son stood on the step ladder and watched. He kept reaching for the hot pan but each time I pulled his hand away and explained why he should not touch the pan. He managed to get past me and touch the pan once, as he said the word "hot!" What did he learn from that experience? He learned a new level of hot (hot pan versus hot food), he learned that I am credible (I meant what I said), and hopefully he learned to heed future warnings.

Children have strong emotions just like adults do, and they should be taught that it is okay to have these emotions and to express their emotions. They get excited and want to run around and scream. They get frustrated and want to cry and fuss. Although kids should express their emotions, they also need to be taught that there is a proper time and place. When my youngest is frustrated about something, I talk to him about the situation to discover the source of the frustration and help him come up with alternative ways to handle the situation. After a minute, if he still needs to express his frustration by fussing or crying, I tell him, "You can fuss all you want in your room." Then I take him to his room, and before closing the door I remind him that he can come out of his room when he is finished fussing. Usually within a couple of minutes, he regains his self-control and exits his room with a good attitude. It is important during these interactions with your kids to set the example of self-control. This is especially difficult when your child has done something wrong, and this is the millionth time you've had to talk to him or her about this behavior. Don't yell or have an emotional outburst. Speak calmly, and have a discussion about the behavior. Talk about what your child did that was wrong, why it was wrong, and what he or she can do differently next time. If you happen to lose your self-control during the interaction, apologize right away and explain that you were wrong for losing your self-control.

Admit your own faults and discuss your own struggles with your kids, especially as they enter the teenage years. I had a conversation not too long ago with my oldest daughter, about having a good attitude. I told her she had to understand how her crabby, grumpy, selfish attitude had resulted in a negative experience in the swimming pool for her dad and siblings. As we talked about how her attitude affects others, I realized that I sometimes get stressed out, act crabby, and have negative interactions with my kids. I asked her if she has been hurt by how I sometimes interact with her. I explained that it takes effort, when feeling stressed for whatever reason, to have positive interactions with people. We discussed how we all need to make a conscious effort not to snap at people when we are feeling grumpy, and treat others the way we want to be treated.

When entering a situation that may prove challenging, discuss with your kids ahead of time what challenges they may face, and strategies to deal with those situations. Be proactive, not reactive.

For example, when we were preparing for a trip to Disney World, we foresaw that even with all the fun, our children would still need a break to recharge and have some calm time. We planned several snack breaks throughout the day. We would lay out a picnic blanket wherever we could find an out of the way spot, have water and snacks, and rest. We also planned a several hour break in the mid-afternoon, when we would leave the park, go back to the hotel, swim in the pool, and have a good meal. Then we would return to the park, refreshed and ready to have more fun. We discussed the plan with the kids ahead of time, explaining why these breaks were important and when we would be taking them.

On a smaller scale, when we took our older kids skiing for the first time, we talked to them about the challenges they might face (frustration in learning to ski, cold hands and feet, waiting in line for the chair lift), and how to deal with each of those challenges. Their first skiing experience was much more enjoyable because they knew what to expect and how to handle those situations.

So many times I hear parents communicating with their kids in ways that just astound me. The parents are reacting in an emotional outburst, not thinking about what kind of message they are communicating or how to teach the child anything. We were on vacation, swimming in the hotel pool. I noticed a mother and her very fussy child interacting at the other end of the pool. The little girl must have been one or maybe even two years old. She was whining incessantly, and the mother kept snapping at her impatiently, saying, "What do you want? Stop it!" The mother wanted to make the fussing stop, and the child wanted her mother's attention. Neither mom nor little girl were getting what they wanted, yet the pattern continued until the little girl burst into tears and the mother roughly picked her up and carried her away in a huff.

During that same vacation, our kids were playing at the playground. A little boy, who was there with his father, fell down and began to cry. He walked over to his dad with his little arms outstretched, and his dad gruffly said, "Stop crying! Brush it off!" Now, I can understand wanting your child to be tough and not overreact to every little bump or scrape. But this little guy needed some comfort from his dad, and all his dad could manage was a cold, detached response.

We live near a lake, and there is a lakeside park we like to visit once in a while. It has a nice fishing dock, and a boardwalk that runs along the shore of the lake. A mom was there on the boardwalk with her young son. She was obviously nervous about him falling off the boardwalk into the water. She repeatedly grabbed him, pulled him away from the railing, and yelled, "No!" At one point I heard her say, "Get back- I don't trust you!"

What would you have done in these three situations? In the first example, dealing with such a young child, it was not effective for the mother to repeatedly ask her child want she wanted. My guess is that this little girl needed some attention, a snack, and a nap, when what her mother wanted to do was lie by the pool and sunbathe. In the second example, the boy needed his father to show that he cared about him. After a few loving and encouraging words, he probably would have been up and playing happily. In the last example, the mother was being reactive, not proactive, and not teaching her son anything constructive. Knowing she was taking her son to a park near the water, she could have explained the rules ahead of time (always hold mommy's hand, no climbing on the railing, etc.) and also the reasons for the rules. Then, if a rule was broken, she could have given a warning and then left the park if it was broken again. That child would quickly learn that the rules are important, and that his mom means what she says!

My daughter remembers a time when we were at a local take out pizza place. We were waiting for our order to be prepared, and were watching an interaction between a mother and her young son. He really wanted a soda, so without asking first, he walked over to the soda display, removed a bottle of soda, and placed it on the counter. Without a word of explanation, the mother picked up the bottle and put it back in the cooler. The son again retrieved a bottle of soda and set it on the counter, and the mother put it back. When, for the third time, the son walked to the soda cooler, the mother's response was to yell "NO", grab her son's arm, and yank him away. There was never any positive communication, no discussion, no explanation. What did the boy learn from that interaction?

My toddler had a runny nose, and when he couldn't readily find a tissue, he proceeded to wipe his nose on his older sister. It would have been easy for me to react by yelling "No!" and grabbing him away, but what would that response teach him? What is needed in that situation is discussion and explanation. It takes more time and effort, but is the only way he will learn not to do it again. I explained that we do not wipe our noses on other people, or on our clothes, or on furniture- only on tissues. I asked him if he would like it if I wiped my nose on him. Of course he responded, "No, that's yucky!" I explained that germs are spread by wiping your nose around, and that germs make people sick. We then talked about what he should do the next time he needs to wipe his nose but can't find a tissue (ask for help). A little while later he came to me and asked me to help him get a tissue for his nose. He had learned the lesson!

Talk to your kids about everything. Explain the reasons behind your actions and choices, so your kids learn how to make good decisions. Stay calm when communicating, so your children can learn from you. Follow through on what you say, so you earn credibility with your kids.

Attitude is Everything

In life it is ironic how often we create much of our own luck, whether good or bad. Bad things happen – that's life, but how you deal with it says a lot about you and how well you are able to teach your children to handle future challenges in their lives. It always amazes me to see how often people with generally negative attitudes seem to have trouble in their lives. It makes me wonder which came first, the poor attitude, or the bad luck. I am firmly convinced that any problem is made more or less severe based on how you choose to respond to it. Never let a situation take control of you and always remember that a sense of humor is an essential survival tool, especially for parents.

I remember many challenging moments that were not in the least bit funny in the moment but great fun to laugh at later on. My four year old daughter fell out of a hammock when we were camping, she split her chin open on a rock and blood was all over her and the ground. Due to our remote location it took us nearly four hours to get her into an emergency room and by then her chin had stopped bleeding. We ended up putting four little stitches in my daughter's chin. You can imagine how we all felt on the long drive back to camp site. We were so tired when we got back to the tent that we didn't even have dinner, and we went straight to bed. Early the next morning we heard cute little girl giggles coming from our daughter's sleeping bag. She had found a mirror and was checking out the doctor's handy work and decided that she looked like a catfish with whiskers (the ends of the suture thread stuck out about a ½" on either side of her chin). Our little girl had let the trauma and frustration of the previous day go and was enjoying her new facial feature. How could we be grumpy when she had set the example of good behavior for us to follow?

Often situations arise that catch us off guard and unprepared. Many times we choose to respond by getting extremely frustrated or even angry. Remember that every action you take is a choice you make for which you are responsible. Teach self control by emulating it yourself. Don't let one bad decision become a string a bad decisions that only makes a problem much bigger than it really has to be. A problem is most often only as big as you make it.

I remember my oldest daughter proudly making strawberry sauce for my wife's birthday cake. She spent hours starting out with fresh strawberries and creating her own little master piece. She filled a beautiful crystal gravy boat with the sauce and while attempting to carry the sauce into the dining room, tripped and dumped the strawberry sauce all over the dining room carpet. The disappointment and stress exploded into all of us: The sauce was wasted, the hours of work were wasted, the chance for an appreciative mother to be impressed was lost, my wife's chance for a few minutes of birthday pleasure were ruined, and the carpet was toast. So what would you do? Would you yell at your daughter and send her off to go cry in her room? The secret was to quickly turn the situation around. We all pitched in to clean up the mess and had another attempt at a birthday party on the back porch about 30 minutes later. There was enough sauce left for my wife to slather her cake with it and when she let out an exaggerated "mmmmm" my daughter lit up like a Christmas tree. The moment was now as positive as you can get and no emotional scars were created. Now we even get to have a little fun teasing my daughter whenever the crystal gravy boat makes an appearance.

Teaching Moments and Spending Time Together

A major component of a child's education that is often overlooked is informal education. Kids are experts at learning from observation. Being aware of this fact will help you to understand that "do as I say, not as I do" doesn't work. Infants learn mostly by observation, so with this knowledge you must model the behavior you expect. Every situation that arises is a learning opportunity whether you have prepared in advance or not. Learn to take advantage of these teaching moments to model good behavior and explain why you expect a certain behavior as much as possible. The more intense the situation, the more powerful the memory will likely be for your child. Make the most of every opportunity to help your child learn the right way. Remember that the easy solution is often the wrong solution.

The more time you spend with your child, the more informal learning opportunities will occur. This is even greater when you can expose your children to different things like going to the science center or the zoo. Teach observation skills and discuss the things your kids see and how they are important or significant. Remember that kids look at the world from an entirely different perspective than adults so don't be disappointed when what they talk about on the way home was what they had for lunch instead of the things you thought were important. Kids will process their memories again and again and will likely recall details and ask questions long after you have forgotten the day altogether.

Some of my fondest memories are of doing simple everyday tasks, like cooking pancakes with my kids. Most kids have a natural desire to want to be involved with everything and are proud whenever they can "help". Look for chances to get you kids engaged in whatever you do, even if it's cleaning the bathroom.

Spending time together should also be about showing your kids who you are and the things you enjoy doing. This not only helps the kids learn about new things but it also helps them to get to know you as a person and build an understanding of you. Good leaders make a point to allow people around them to get to know them well. As you get to know a person you build understanding with them which in turn builds trust. The more people know about you, the more understanding they can have with you. The key here is to be proud of who you are and actively show what you are passionate about.

A leadership concept that may be helpful to consider is that every person has portions of their personality that they show openly and portions that they prefer to keep private. Within these areas we each have tendencies which we express consciously and unconsciously. As a general rule, effective leaders have nearly 80% of their personality in the consciously public area which allows those that follow them to see who they are and easily know what is important to them. People that choose to have larger portions of their personality held private are more difficult to get to know and are more difficult to develop understanding with. Help your kids understand you by spending time with them, especially if you are the type of person that has a more reserved personality.

Some great examples, written by my wife, Maya

Cooking together is a great way to spend time with your kids. Get them involved from the beginning of the process (meal planning and shopping) all the way to the end (cooking and serving the meal). Use meal planning as an opportunity to reinforce a balanced diet and good eating habits. Shopping can be a great time to practice reading and math. While cooking, kids can learn about cooking methods, units of measurement, how to read a recipe, etc. Serving their creation to family members can foster good relationships between the kids, when the siblings appreciate the hard work of other siblings. My oldest two children are now able to work together to make a meal, with no help!

Shopping with kids can be a real challenge, but if you get them involved in the process, then they are less likely to get bored and cause trouble. Because I have four children, we get two carts. My oldest pushes my youngest in one cart. I push the second cart, and my middle two children do the shopping. They take turns reading the list and looking for the items. If there are different sized packages of the same item, the kids figure out which package size is most economical. Just for fun, the kids try to keep track of how much the items cost, and whoever is the closest to the actual amount when we check out gets a small prize. Shopping can be fun and educational!

Has there ever been a time when you've been trying to get a project done around the house, and you keep getting interrupted by your kids? I've been there plenty of times, and the best remedy for that situation is to get your kids involved! My son helps his dad change the oil and rotates the tires on the van, and they have worked together to build three loft beds, and several wooden shelves. The girls help me clean out the refrigerator, organize the closets, and sort through our home schooling work to make portfolios. All the kids pitch in when it is time to wash and wax the vehicles. We all worked together to design and build a big tree fort (48 feet long and 12 feet high) It's a tree fort that looks like a pirate ship!

Sometimes it's all about having fun. My oldest son is a Cub Scout, and every year the scouts have a different theme. One year the theme was the Yukon Gold Rush. We recreated a few of the Cub Scout activities with our own children at home, including making a kid-powered dog sled, and fishing for red "snappers" (mouse traps painted red). The kids also enjoy pretending to be fish, when mom and dad go fishing from the tree fort using gummy worms as bait. We like making treasure hunts for each other, with written clues that lead to a prize at the end. We practice outdoor skills with the kids, by teaching them how to make a fire without matches, and how to navigate the neighborhood using a map and compass. My oldest daughter loves catching critters of all kinds, and my husband and daughter spend time together recreating habitats in tanks for the critters. My husband and kids made a water rocket out of a soda bottle that they pressurized with a bicycle pump- it flew over 50 feet in the air! There are a lot of books available that contain simple science experiments and projects.

Taking unique vacations are a great way to spend time teaching your kids new things. Every year we go camping for two weeks on a lake in the mountains. Camping in a tent, on an island, with no bathroom or other comforts, is a great place to connect with your kids and provide them with unique experiences. During our annual camping trip the kids get to go swimming, water skiing, mountain climbing, canoeing, and fishing. This year something new was added- scuba diving! Last winter we took our oldest two children snow skiing for the first time- they loved it and talked about skiing with such excitement, now our third child wants to try it. On a recent weekend trip to the mountains, we took our oldest three children white water kayaking. These unique experiences not only create wonderful family memories, but they also give the kid's confidence.

Luckily, we have some great resources within a couple hours' drive from home. We are able to take the kids to the zoo, the aquarium, the ballet, the marionette theater, and various museums. All of these activities can be time for fun as well as great learning experiences.

Take time to talk to your kids to explain difficult concepts and take advantage of teaching moments. We love having family dinners around the dining room table, because it gives us the opportunity to talk about what is going on in our daily lives, as well as events that are occurring around the world. My husband loves to talk about a math or science concept, and how it relates to everyday life. We talk to the kids about the dangers they face (drugs, dangerous drivers, bad guys), and how to be prepared to face those dangers. Woven into these discussions is the theme of good decision making, because everything in life is a choice, and making good choices is critical to being successful.

Have Fun Together

I enjoy spending time with my kids, and most of all I enjoy having fun with my kids. While not everyday can be a trip to Disney World, we can certainly have fun while we are working. We enjoy making up silly games to play when traveling in the car. I'll start by saying a word and the kids have to come up with a word that starts with the last letter of my word. Many times we end up giggling about words that aren't real or are spelled incorrectly. An example would be as follows:

- I say "boot"
- One of the kids says "tiger"
- I say "rattlesnake"
- One of the kids says "kite"

Then we all giggle because the word rattlesnake ends with a silent "e" so they need to come up with a word that starts with an "e" instead of a word that starts with a "k".

In our daily routine I look for ways to play with the kids or tease them in a silly way. One morning I set the table for breakfast with the smallest spoon in the house at my oldest daughters place. When she saw what I had done, she rolled her eyes and asked for a bigger spoon. At this point everyone was at the table so I said, "Sure!" and brought out the biggest serving spoon in the house. My daughter gave me a few more eye rolls, and then despite her best effort to prevent it, a smile crept into position. I knew I had her and I managed to keep a poker face for a minute or two. Everyone had a good giggle and then I got up and gave her a normal sized spoon.

One of the stories the kids like to tell was of me teasing my oldest son. He had asked me to cut up his dinner for him and I pretended not to understand what he was asking me to do. I asked him to show me what he wanted me to do, then I would only repeat exactly what he had done and nothing more. He was trying to show me with his hands how to cut his hot dog so I made the same motions with my hands. When he got frustrated I ended up karate chopping his hot dog and it actually broke in half where I hit it. The other kids thought this was great fun but I could see it had gone on a little too long so I quickly cut his dinner exactly how he wanted it to be. Now that he is a little older he encourages me to play this trick on the younger kids, because he appreciates the humor now.

At the end of mealtime the kids ask to be excused. We make a point to respond immediately and tell them to clear their dishes, clean their hands and face and then come back to the table for "the sticky test". If we can find a sticky spot on their hands or face we get to tickle them. While they enjoy playing along, they learn very quickly how to be efficient at washing up after mealtime.

I make a point to have some fun time everyday with the kids. We may sit and read a book or have hallway races. We might make up a silly game or have a wild wrestling match. Sometimes I find the kids have prepared something for me, like a puppet show or music recital. Whatever it is that you do with your kids, make the effort and make the most of every opportunity.

Daily Schedule

You will often find that there don't seem to be enough hours in the day for all of the activities that you need to complete. When you find that you are consistently struggling to keep up, it's time to implement a formal schedule to help you stay organized and focus on the key things that are your first priorities each day. Since we home school our children, it is necessary to have a schedule to be sure that the kids get all of their school work done, while also having time to do chores and play. Children thrive when they have a consistent schedule. They need to get enough sleep and have consistent meal times. They need to have time to do all of their daily tasks (morning routine, meals, homework, chores, play, bedtime routine) and they like to know what is coming up next. They also need to learn how to use their time wisely.

How to construct a schedule, written by my wife, Maya

How do you go about constructing a schedule? There are five main steps.

First, write a list of the things that you need to do each day. Focus on tasks that are essential- you absolutely must do them every day. The concept here is to understand what are the few most important things that must be completed each day and each week. Then estimate how much time it takes to do each task. Here is a portion of my list, as an example:

Morning routine (make bed, shower, dress) 30 minute

Breakfast (prep, eat, clean up) 45 minutes

Individual school time with each child (1 hour each)- 3 hours

Lunch (prep, eat, clean up)- 1 hour

Housecleaning- 1 hour

To-do list items- 30 minutes

Dinner (prep, eat, clean up)- 1.5 hours

Second, do a time study. For one week, write down everything you do and how long you spend doing each thing. Look at things you spend your time on, and compare those tasks to the list you made in the first step. If there are things that take up your time but are not included in your list of important tasks, try and find a way to reduce or eliminate them. When I did my time study, I found that one area that used up my time was looking for items that I needed to complete my daily tasks. I realized that in order to eliminate the time spent looking for things; I needed to build into my schedule a daily time to organize my house.

Third, compare your actual times to your time estimates from the first step, and adjust accordingly. I discovered when I did my time study that although I had planned only 30 minutes each for the breakfast and lunch routines, in actuality I used 45 minutes for breakfast and an entire hour for lunch.

Fourth, determine the time of day each task must be done. Some tasks must be done at a certain time of day, like your morning routine, bedtime routine, and sleep. Other tasks are determined by when other things happen, like having lunch at a certain time because that is when Dad can be available. Some things are flexible, like when to shower or do chores, and some tasks are better to do while a toddler is napping, or before all of the kids get up in the morning.

Fifth, put all of the tasks on individual index cards or sticky notes, with each card equivalent to a one hour time block. You can move the cards around until you determine the best order in which to accomplish your tasks. Then write or type out your schedule. Be sure to save the index cards or sticky notes, for the next time you need to re-design your schedule. If you are comfortable using a spreadsheet program, you can do this step right on your computer, instead of using the index cards. As you construct your schedule, be sure to leave some empty space where you don't have anything scheduled, just in case unexpected things come up. Also, build in a few minutes, a couple of times a day, to assess your progress and that of your kids, to be sure things are getting done on time. I have a check-in time with my kids just after lunch, to be sure they are on track to finish their school work on time, and another check-in time at the end of the day before dinner prep begins. Check-in times are especially important when you have multiple children doing a lot of school work independently.

As you develop your daily work plan, have each member of the house do the same. Teach your kids how to go through the same steps you used above to construct their own schedules. When I went through this process with my older three children, we discovered that a lot of time is wasted looking for pencils, erasers, markers, and whatever other school supplies are needed during our homeschool day. Together, we came up with a solution- we made up a school supply box for each child, with a list of items written on an index card taped to the inside of the box. Every Sunday evening, it is part of my kids' bedtime routines to go through their school supply boxes to be sure they are complete before the school week begins.

You can put all schedules into one master spreadsheet. Print it out and hang it up so everyone can see what everyone else is doing at a particular moment in time. This has been helpful to make our homeschool run more efficiently. If one child finishes his or her school work early, he or she can easily look at the schedule to see if a sibling is available to play, or is involved in school work or chores.

Here are some details about our schedule that you may or may not want to incorporate into yours. I get up at least an hour ahead of the kids, so that I have enough time to do my morning routine before the kids get up. Having time focused time with my husband is extremely important, so I have built into my schedule a half hour in the morning and a half hour in the evening when he is supposed to get my undivided attention (we have a toddler so that is still a work in progress). The kids and I have designed their schedules so that our toddler has some focused time with each sibling every day. The children's schedules allow them to get all of their school work done, and includes time for chores, play, and other activities. Along with breakfast, lunch, and dinner, I have built in morning and afternoon snack times. Outside play time after lunch is an important part of each day, as is evening quiet play time while I prepare dinner. One of our favorite times of the day is evening family time, which usually consists of wild time with Daddy (wrestling and Nerf gun battles are common) and then calm time when Daddy reads to the kids.

On the schedule I have a time for both a morning routine and a bedtime routine. For the kids, I have typed and posted both of these routines in their rooms, so they can remember exactly what they need to do each morning and evening. One of the rules in our house is that we must be able to walk through a room at all times. We explain to the kids that it is important, in case of emergency that we can run through a room in the dark without tripping over anything. That is why cleaning the bedroom is built into my kids' morning and bedtime routines. During each routine, the kids must clean their "messiest horizontal surface". If the bedroom floor is messiest, it gets picked up. If the top of the dresser is in chaos, it gets cleaned. Copies of these routines have been included in the appendix.

Your child's bedtime routing should be simple and consistent. Stick to a few key events that you can do every night- put away toys, pajamas on, brush teeth, story, song, sleep. The bedtime routing is parent directed, not child dictated. You, the parent, decide what time to start the routine. You decide how many stories to read or songs to sing. You decide the order in which to do the routine. To maintain consistency, write out and post the bedtime routine so your child knows what to do and in what order. For a child who does not yet know how to read, you can make a picture chart. Around the time my youngest child turned three, he began to fight me over nap time. He would be playing after he ate his lunch, I would say, "naptime", and he would get really upset. I made a picture chart for him of his entire day, which is hanging up in his room. To make the chart, I took photos of him doing the things he normally does each day- eating, playing, napping, etc. I printed and laminated the photos, and hung them in the correct order on a sheet of poster board. I made a large arrow that he can move around on the poster board, with some blue tacky stuff on the back to make it stick. When it is time to transition from one thing to another, we stand in front of his picture chart, and he moves the arrow down the chart to the next activity. He can see what is coming up next, and he feels like he has control because he moves the arrow to the next activity. For kids who are learning about time, you could even put times on the chart for when each event is supposed to occur, or how many minutes will be spent on each activity.

After you have constructed your master schedule, do another time study and adjust your schedule as necessary. Try not to get frustrated when life doesn't fit into your master schedule. Remember that life is always in flux and flexibility is a necessity. We hardly ever have what I would call a "normal" week- between doctor appointments, field trips and social events with our homeschooling group, visits from grandparents and other relatives- we are always adjusting our schedule. It seems as though just as I get my schedule settled, something changes- naptime for my toddler shifts, holidays come, baseball season begins…and I have to rework my schedule…again.

Having a consistent schedule is important, but being flexible with that schedule is equally important. For example, on nights when the kids have an evening activity such as Tae Kwon Do or a Cub Scout meeting, we allow the kids to stay up an extra half hour to allow time to spend with Daddy. We feel that having that Daddy time is more important than the half hour of sleep lost, and the kids actually sleep better when the evening routine includes that time with Dad.

Your standard workday must include enough flexibility to address needs as they come up. It is best to start with a goal of scheduling no more than 50% of the hours of your day and remember to leave unscheduled time in between scheduled events to allow enough flexibility to deal with life in the real world. Stay focused and committed to the plan that you have established and expect others to do the same. Spend the remainder of your work day as needed and seek to gradually increase the percentage of your time you can successfully schedule and stick with.

Remember to include at least 30 minutes of scheduled time each day for one-time actions to improve the structure and accountability in the problem areas. This is the prime time way to make improvements to your daily life but focus on very small projects you can complete in 30 min or less. If you choose a small re-organizing project, (such as a drawer, a toy box or a shelf) take a picture of the finished project. Be sure to put responsibilities in place on who is responsible to keep it looking this way and how often you will be coming by to inspect what you expect (usually daily). If you don't follow-up with these inspections and consequences things will simply go back to whatever is easiest in the short term (which is rarely what is best for the long term).

In addition to having a daily schedule, it is important to keep track of events that occur on a weekly or monthly basis. We have a dry erase calendar hanging on the wall of our kitchen, where everyone can see it. Each month I update the calendar with all of our social events, field trips, sports and scouting activities, etc. If you have many family members with different activities, they can be color coded so each family member's activities are a particular color. I meet with the kids at the beginning of each week to go over the activities, so everyone knows what is coming up that week. My husband and I usually set aside some time on Thursday evening to discuss the weekend plan- what social events, to-do items, and other activities are going on that weekend. All of this planning allows us to use our time more effectively.

Chores

Housekeeping is not complicated to do but it is difficult to get everyone to contribute. It starts with the expectation that everyone has a responsibility to assist in maintaining the orderliness and cleanliness of the house. Explain the things that must be done and how everyone can help each day. Any time your kids spend supporting you versus making more work for you pays you back two to one. Begin with including different housekeeping activities in everyone's daily schedule. Rotating these chores gives everyone a chance to learn each of the tasks. Your children need to be trained in the chores you expect them to do, and you need to have achievable expectations for each person. Your kids should present to you what they have done and you should be sure to recognize their good work and avoid being nit-picky. If their work is really sloppy, don't lecture. Just be straight with them that more effort is needed and plan some time to discuss your expectations and go through the training again. Be sure to engage the more experienced kids to help perform inspections as they get more confident in their abilities. Always remember that you must live by the same standards you set for the kids.

Many problems arise from lack of understanding the expectations (lack of knowledge or lack of skills), and lack of desire to do the work (lack of will). The simple answer is that you need to teach your children how to clean up before you can expect them to do it on their own. Start by working together on small daily chores that are unique to them and their possessions. Once your are sure that you have provided enough training and support to prevent having issues due to lack of knowledge or lack of skill, you have eliminated the potential for most excuses that could be launched at you. Any gaps in performance that remain are likely due to a lack of will to do the task. If this is the barrier you are facing, then it's time for some behavior modification, which will be addressed in more detail in another section. If you find they consistently have trouble cleaning up toys, put the toys that are the problem in storage for a week. After the week have a discussion about how to ensure these toys get put away properly and then bring them back to see what happens. If problems continue, it may be time for a generous donation to needy kids in your area.

How to construct a chore schedule, written by my wife, Maya

I mentioned in the last section that we set aside a time for chores in our daily routine. Even if you have a full-time housekeeper, there will be some daily chores that you and your children need to do. I have struggled for years with keeping my house clean and neat. It is difficult to keep up with the demands of being a wife, mother, and teacher. But recently I have discovered a method that works well for me, and I will describe it step-by-step. It comes from a homeschooling friend with a very large family. First, go room by room with a large pad of paper. Make a list of every job that must be done in that room. Write down an estimate of how long each job takes, and how often each job needs to be done (daily, weekly, twice monthly, monthly, quarterly). Also make a note of who, besides you, is able to do each job or be trained to do each job. Here is my list for our kitchen:

Job	How long	How often	Who*
Vacuum	15 minutes	2X per week	K, R, N
Mop	15 minutes	Weekly	K, R, N
Empty dishwasher	15 minutes	daily	K, R, N
Organize cabinets	30 minutes	monthly	K, R, N, with mom
Wash windows	30 minutes	Every 6 months	K, R, N, with mom
Wood oil on cabinets	30 minutes	Quarterly	K, R
Clean out fridge	30 minutes	Monthly	Mom
Clean toaster	15 minutes	2X per month	Mom
Clean microwave	15 minutes	2X per month	Mom
Clean oven	15 minutes	Monthly	Mom
Disinfect countertops	15 minutes	2X per month	Mom
Wash highchair	15 minutes	Weekly	K, R
Take out trash	5 minutes	2X per week	K, R, N
Take out recycling	5 minutes	Weekly	K, R, N
Wipe door, light switches, baseboards	30 minutes	Quarterly	K, R, N

** K, R, and N stand for the names of my oldest three kids*

Next, tabulate all of the daily, weekly, twice monthly, monthly, and quarterly jobs, and assign each job to a person. This step is more easily done if all of the information is entered into a spreadsheet, since you can use a spreadsheet to sort by room, job, person, time interval, etc.

Finally, make a chore calendar. I use my chore spreadsheet to fill in my chore calendar one month at a time. Then print the calendar and post it. It's amazing how much difference even just thirty minutes a day of help from everyone can make. My husband recently came home from work and made a positive comment about the fresh vacuum marks on the carpet. Boy, did that bring a smile to my face!

Some parents struggle when trying to determine what tasks their children can do. Don't underestimate the jobs your kids can handle, especially when they are trained to do those jobs. Some of the jobs done by my kids are-sweeping, vacuuming, mopping, dusting, polishing furniture, doing laundry, cleaning bathrooms, washing windows…the list of what they are capable of goes on and on.

Kids can begin to do chores as soon as they can reach for a toy. Hold your baby in your lap and help him or her pick up toys and put them away. Even your youngest children can be involved in doing the laundry. A one year old who can stand next to you in the laundry room can put items in the dryer as you hand them one by one. A two year old can sort clothes into baskets. A three year old can learn to fold washcloths and small towels as you talk about shapes and colors. A four year old can learn to fold shirts and pants, as you talk about folding into halves and quarters. When my youngest daughter was five, she began folding and putting away her own laundry, with a little help and encouragement from her older sister. My toddler loves to help collect the dirty laundry from the bathroom hampers. He has so much fun pushing the hampers down the hall to the laundry room. He sits up on the dryer and puts the clothes in the washer as I hand them to him. He pours in the soap and pushes the buttons to start the washer. He puts the wet clothes into the dryer as I hand them to him and pushes the buttons to start the dryer. When it comes time to fold the laundry, my oldest daughter sorts the clothes into individual laundry baskets for each child, which are identified by a certain color of ribbon tied around the handle. I have taught my oldest three children to fold and put away their own laundry. My youngest child helps me fold and put away his clothes. They all pitch in to help fold towels, sheets, and blankets. The youngest kids fold the washcloths and pillowcases, and the oldest kids work together to fold the larger items. Sometimes we turn it into a game by having laundry folding races!

When my oldest two children were 11 and 9, I trained them how to clean the bathroom. First, I had them watch and take detailed notes as I cleaned my bathroom. They wrote down what to do, what supplies to use, and the order in which to do things. My oldest child typed and printed the notes, and then they worked together to clean the other two bathrooms in the house. I inspected their work and made suggestions for improvement. After a few months of practice, I can now rely on my oldest daughter and son to clean the kids' bathrooms on their own.

I previously mentioned that keeping their bedrooms picked up is a chore that my kids work on twice daily, during their morning and bedtime routines. We feel it is important that the kids keep their rooms clean. It shows that they have respect for their belongings and appreciate them. Having a clean bedroom allows them to move freely about their rooms without tripping over things. They are also able to find things when they need them. Sometimes cleaning up their rooms can seem like a big job, and to help them put things away where they belong, we use photos. Work with your child to get his or her bedroom the way you expect it to be. Then take pictures of the toys on the shelves, the top of the dresser, the bed, the closet, and any other area you expect your child to keep clean. Print and laminate the pictures to make it easy for your child to clean up to your expectations.

To-Do List (written by my wife, Maya)

Does it seem like your to-do list has hundreds of action items on it and that it gets longer everyday? I have a list of action items, which is separate from my household chore list, and includes both one time action items and ongoing things that need to be done. My to-do list is in a spreadsheet, with the following columns: "importance, category, action item, notes, who, by when". Each action item gets a number, with "1" being most important and "5" being least important. I assign a due date for each action item based on its importance. The due date is always a Saturday, so if I do not complete an action item during the week, it gets included in the weekend plan. I have found that it is important to try and work on my to-do list each day. On my daily schedule (included in the appendix), you will see that I have included a thirty minute time slot each day to work on to-do list action items. It is important to choose a time of day that works best for you, like before the kids get up in the morning, or during the toddler's nap time.

There will always be things that come up week to week that are not in your monthly action item plan. When assigning due dates to action items, don't over schedule, to allow time to take care of those unplanned action items.

Everyday is a New Opportunity – Make the Most of It

As you begin to implement your plans, recognize that you will need to start small, win a small victory and celebrate a little bit each day. The key is to build a strong foundation for the future and be consistent. Make sure to recognize your children's positive contributions each day and make it a goal to have more than half of the communication with your children be positive each day.

Think of these positive comments as investments in an emotional bank account. Make sure these are legitimate and never condescending. Learn to catch you child at their best behavior everyday and make these investments in your relationship count. Whenever you punish or scold a child you make a withdrawal. You need to discipline in order to teach your child correct behavior. In fact, the word discipline comes from the Latin word *disciplina* which means "to teach". How you handle the discipline defines how big of an emotional withdrawal you make. Learn to speak calmly, clearly, and respectfully to explain why the behavior is wrong and what the correct behavior should have been. Set a goal for this communication to last less than one minute and then focus on something else. This will get the point across while making a minimum withdrawal.

When your account runs negative, the trust your child has for you becomes strained and every interaction becomes a battle. Always remember that you are the parent and it is your responsibility to take the high road and teach your child by setting the example of loving and respectful behavior, especially during emotional moments. It is during these moments that people expose who they really are. Stay cool, think before acting, and take a break if necessary by having the child do a time out (usually 1 minute per year of age works well). Remember, they are learning from your actions, especially when the pressure is on.

Many times when things aren't going well the key is simply to break the cycle of behavior by doing something different – anything different. I like taking kids for a walk when this happens, even in the middle of the night if necessary. When I was a camp counselor we were told during the first days at camp with the new kids, that many would get homesick and want to go home. We were instructed to distract these kids no matter what we had to do for the first twenty-four hours. Usually after this amount of time they were willing to at least "try" staying for one more day and then they felt fine.

I had one eleven year old boy that was crying so uncontrollably he could not speak. After nearly thirty minutes of attempting to get him to talk, I took him for a walk around the camp jogging track. This still wasn't working so we turned it into a jog. After nearly two hours he was so tired he couldn't even remember what the issue was. As a result, he stayed with me the whole summer and asked me if I would be his counselor again next year. Unfortunately, I had to go back to college and wasn't able to come back the next year, but I do have some really great memories of that summer.

Needless to say after two hours on the jogging track I was worn out in everyway you could imagine. I look back on that as indoctrination training at dad camp. After pushing through that evening of emotional meltdown, no issue with my children has even come close. As a result, I have occasionally reminded myself of that day and said secretly to myself "this is nothing compared to that day". Remember to keep things in perspective and realize that most problems are really only as big as you make them out to be.

If you find yourself dealing with a total meltdown when you are out in public and you are not able to leave the area at the immediate moment (like on an airplane), explain this to your child. If she can't stop crying and you need her to stop right away try giving her a lollypop to break the cycle and change the mood. Talk with her calmly while she is eating the lollypop, and most times the crisis is over before the lollypop is gone.

Behavior modification

How often do you expect your kids to obey? All of the time? Sometimes? Never? Whatever your expectations, your children will live up to them. We have a slogan at work; you will achieve the level of performance that you demonstrate you are committed to achieving. While this is an awkwardly worded slogan it very accurately wraps up a key concept of leadership – seeing is believing. If you show your passion for staying calm, speaking respectfully, and always doing the right thing, people will listen to what you have to say. If you can teach others to see what you see when you walk into a messy room and to feel about it the way you feel about it, they will voluntarily clean it up. This is so, not out of compliance with your rules, but out of commitment to the plans you have developed together.

The significance of this concept cannot be overstated. Compliance happens regretfully out of fear of consequences. Compliance is somehow universally unpopular and will not happen when you aren't there watching. In fact, you can bet that most people will make a point to fall short of compliance when the opportunity to get away with it comes along. In how many movies have you found yourself cheering when the underdog revolted against the rules? Compliance should not be the long term expectation unless you are running a jailhouse. The goal should be to help your children understand the reasons why tasks are important and when they see the wisdom and your commitment to living by the same standards you can achieve a commitment from them to do the same.

When things don't go as planned, it is extremely important to know what the root cause is. A handy method is to ask five "why" questions in series. Why was the milk on the floor? Because I was rushing. Why were you rushing? Because the baby was crying. Why was the baby crying? Because he was hungry. Why was he hungry? Because I was an hour late feeding him. The root cause here turned out to be a late feeding. Once the root cause is understood, you can begin working on corrective actions. When you are dealing with attempting to modify the behavior of your children, you can make the five "why" questions into a game. Here is an example of a conversation I had with one of my children. "Why did your sister fall down?" "Because she tripped on my toys." "Why were the toys on the floor?" "Because I didn't put them away." "Why didn't you put them away?" "Because the shelf is too messy and there is no room." "Why is the shelf messy?" "Because the other toys aren't put away properly." "Why aren't they put away properly?" Because I don't know where they are supposed to go." Once the root cause was understood, we developed a corrective action. In this case, I worked with the child to organize the toys on the shelf properly, took pictures of the shelf, and posted the pictures near the shelf she could refer to them during the cleanup process.

If things continue to not go well, you need to determine if the child doesn't understand how or what to do, or if she just doesn't want to do it. If lack of understanding is the cause, then more training and visual reminders are the answer. If she just doesn't want to do it, then it's time for behavior modification.
The cold hard fact is that kids (and adults) will do what they believe to be in their short term best interest, often without thinking it through at all. Many kids act or react based purely on emotion, which can be drastically different from day to day. This is often what the child feels like at this particular moment and nothing more. This shouldn't be viewed as good or bad but simply the way the child feels. Help explain the context of his actions and how acting only on feelings may impact others. Always dicsuss the reasons why his actions were good or bad and help him see the way others will likely see his actions. Have patience and work together on reasonable daily expectations instead of jumping to conclusions about his actions, and remember to apply the rule of understanding mentioned earlier.

In general, opinions about new expectations are formed instantly and new behaviors become habits with lightning speed. All of this is based on attitude and understanding at the time the new expectation is created. Once new habits are formed, they are hard to break. This is why daily inspections and feedback are so important. If incorrect behavior takes root and behavior modification becomes necessary, you must ensure consistent negative consequences of a greater magnitude than the perceived benefit of the current behavior if you are going to convince a person to change.

Consequences contain three elements: Timeliness, significance, and certainty. If you want to change behavior you need to establish expectations and provide whatever appropriate training that is required for the person to understand how to meet your expectations. Once the new expectation is in place, you must inspect for whatever expectations you put in place, and do this consistently. These inspections must be daily in most cases (timely). The person needs to know 100% for sure (certainty) that you will do these inspections. Finally, the person needs to know that if they fail to meet these expectations that they can definitely expect consequences that are of greater negative (significance) than any benefit they can gain by not performing to your expectations.

Let's consider the above example of my child leaving her toys on the floor even though she has been told each day to clean them up. The likely outcome is that the child isn't going to change behavior without consequences. Start setting your expectations by explaining the reasons why you have the expectation that toys must be cleaned up before bedtime. Calmly explain the reasons why leaving toys on the floor is not allowed (toys get stepped on and broken, people could trip and fall down, doors can be blocked etc.). Work together to determine how and where the toys should be put away, and take pictures of the shelf or room once the toys are put away properly. Next, agree on the inspection process such as checking that the toys are put away as seen in the pictures just before bedtime each day. Then begin a trial period to allow time for new habits to form. For a week, work with the child during clean up, and then do the inspection together. Discuss the process to reinforce the expectations. Eventually the child should complete the cleanup and inspection herself, asking for help when needed.

Make adjustments to your expectations over time as your child's abilities improve. Remember that it is much better to require your child to clean up half of her toys while you help and have her feel good about the experience, than it would be for you to either do it all for her or yell at her for not doing it entirely on her own. Consider having young children be responsible for one small area (one toy box or one shelf) to allow your child to experience being responsible and held accountable to your standards for something on a daily basis. Tell your child how proud you are and how her actions help the family.

Once you reinforce this success, you can expand the scope of responsibility for each child a little at a time. Remember to focus on areas that they will feel ownership of first such as their own toys, books, and clothes. As your children grow, you can expand their chores into areas that benefit the entire family such as helping with laundry, dishes or the trash. Always remember to adjust your daily plan to include a few minutes for inspection and feedback for each area of responsibility for each child. As the kids become more skilled in handling these daily responsibilities you can move the inspections from daily to weekly and then eventually change them to informal inspections on the fly. Be careful to always live by the same standard you expect of your kids.

If you do this every day without failing, you will establish a clear understanding of the expectations. If the child becomes defiant and simply refuses to do her part, you must apply the negative consequences that are greater than the benefit gained by not cleaning up. Always let the child know what the consequence will be in advance and explain the reasons why the consequences are appropriate at the first signs of trouble. Don't make up a punishment in the heat of the moment. In this case, you could try taking some of the problem toys away for a few days to reduce the time and effort necessary to clean up. When your child begins to perform the clean-up better and more consistently, reward her by bringing back the toys you took away. If the problem continues through several cycles of this method, you may simply need to donate some excess toys to reduce the clutter.

If any of the three elements of your consequence is not present you will not likely succeed in driving change. The consequences you produce must be significant, definite, and immediate to be effective. If you communicate your expectations, provide adequate training, and consistently follow up, you are on the right path. If this follow-up is daily, it will be seen as immediate. If the expectations are age appropriate, firm, and consistent they will be seen as definite. If the repercussions of failing to meet expectations are seen as significant and you stand your ground, you will ultimately succeed in changing behavior. Be consistent about your expectations. Don't change the rules or give in just because you are tired, stressed out, away from home, or have visitors. Once change has occurred, celebrate the success and make sure to maintain the standards. Never let things slip back to old behavior as you will only need to repeat the behavior modification process, which is difficult and time consuming.

One area of frustration for many parents is mealtime. Do not negotiate with your children for what they will eat and not eat. I have heard so many parents negotiating with their children over how much they have to eat, saying "Just five more bites and then you can be done." Create simple rules that the kids can understand and stick to them. Meal time needs to be a time for the family to come together to relax and talk about the day's events, not a time for conflict and confrontation. We have one simple rule that eliminates the stress and negotiation. When mealtime comes, we put a small amount of each item on the child's plate. Remember that it is better to have the child ask for more than to waste food because you gave too large a serving. We leave it to the kids to eat what they want and not eat what they don't want. These are the expectations: We don't force them to eat, and they don't complain about what is on their plate. Our kids can choose to eat everything on their plates, only part of what is on their plates, or nothing. The child can be "all done" at any time with the understanding that they will not have any further food until the next regular meal, unless everything on the plate is eaten.

We have always found the kids learn to eat a little bit of everything in order to earn the right for seconds of the things they like the most. They know the rule and understand the consequences for their choices. We do choose to make exceptions sometimes, if we have visitors over, or if we are at someone else's house for a meal, or if we are having something new. Several studies indicate that young children express preference for foods they recognize, not necessarily foods they like the taste of. It takes tasting an item a dozen or more times before it gets recognized, so keep trying and start early. My suggestion is to develop simple expectations and discuss why they are important with your kids. Make sure you are consistent each night and hold all kids to the same rules. Always remember, your kids will gratefully eat whatever you give them when they get hungry.

Some great examples, written by my wife, Maya

I involve my kids in the weekly meal planning, allowing each child to plan one dinner each week with my guidance. The kids learn about planning meals with nutrition in mind, and they get to look forward to having one meal during the week that they especially like. We also involve the kids in cooking meals as much as possible. They learn how to cut up fruits and vegetables, how to follow a recipe, how to test food for doneness, how to mix things sufficiently, and how to deviate from a recipe to add their own flair. My oldest daughter is now to the point where she can surprise us with a special lasagna dinner, one of my husband's favorites, with no help from me!

Some parents think that once they have a baby, it becomes necessary to baby proof their entire house. We agree that it is important to protect children from danger, and because of that you will find outlet covers in all unused outlets of our house, and a fireplace screen in our fireplace. We don't leave scissors or sharp knives around, and all cleaning supplies are kept in an upper cabinet, away from curious hands. However, you will not find that we have removed fragile decorations, stereo equipment, computers, or nice books out of reach. We feel it is important to teach the kids that there are certain things that they are not allowed to touch, such as Mommy's decorations and Daddy's books, and certain things they are welcome to play with, like their own books and toys.

I have a beautiful lighted Christmas village that my husband has given to me, piece by piece, over the years. We were setting up our Christmas decorations, and my youngest child had just started walking. He toddled over to the shelf on which the Christmas village was set up, and was just reaching up to touch one of the lit-up buildings. I responded with a firm "NO", pulled his hand away, and explained why he was not allowed to touch the fragile village. A minute later he crept back over to the shelf and touched one of the buildings. I slapped his hand and repeated "NO". It took five hand slaps until he chose to comply. I think he understood the expectation, but he was testing to see if I would stand firm and be consistent.

Removing those fragile items from his reach would have also removed the opportunity to teach him about boundaries, obedience, and respect for other people's belongings. Teach your kids about expectations and consequences when they are young. Better for them to learn the lesson early in life, rather than have trouble later when it comes to job performance, marriage challenges, and raising their own kids.

Don't assume that your toddler isn't old enough to comprehend what you mean. Don't just say "NO", explain why the answer is no. While at my younger daughter's soccer game, my youngest child, who was about two year old at the time, went onto the soccer field during the game. We retrieved him from the field, showed him the painted line, told him not to cross the line, and explained why (because he might get hit with the ball or run into by a player, and get hurt). He walked up to the line many times after that, but he did not cross that line again. There was another child of a similar age nearby who repeatedly went onto the soccer field. His dad kept saying no, grabbing his arm, and yanking him back, but not explaining to him why it was not okay to go onto the field. The father finally had to pick up his child in exasperation and walk away with a fussy, wiggling kid. Taking time to explain takes more effort in the moment, but in the long run kids will understand the why behind your boundaries. They will trust you. If there comes a time when you don't have time to explain due to an emergency or some other reason, your kids will trust that there must be a reason, and comply without the need for an explanation.

An example of this occurred when the kids and I were over at a friend's house, and all of our children were playing in the back yard while my friend and I talked. A strange man pulled into my friend's driveway, got out of his vehicle, and began to wander around in the yard. I told the kids to go inside right away, and my own children obeyed immediately. My friend's children wanted an explanation of why they couldn't stay outside for another few minutes. It turned out to be nothing- as it turned out; the man was there for a legitimate reason and posed no threat to us or the kids. But if the man had bad intentions, my children would have been safe, and my friend's kids would have been in harm's way.

It is important to be consistent with expectations and discipline, and it is equally important to use understanding in the disciplining of your children. Recently we had some friends and their children over for dinner. When they arrived my toddler got so excited, he ran over to my friend and hit her. Normally, if one of the kids hits someone, the consequence is a spanking and room time (see further explanation below). But in this case, I realized that my toddler was not intentionally trying to hurt my friend. He got excited, lost his self control, and hit. In that circumstance, I talked to him about what he had done, and how to handle the excitement in a different way. He did not receive the same consequences as if he had hit in anger or frustration. Because I understood my child's intentions, I was able to adjust the consequences accordingly.

Consequences for misbehavior should be determined ahead of time, with your spouse. Do not wait until you are in the middle of a conflict to figure out what the consequence for a particular misbehavior will be. It may be helpful for the child to write out his common misbehaviors and the consequences for each. Discipline should be about teaching, not punishing! You are trying to teach your child what is acceptable behavior, and what is not. Your child needs to understand what he has done wrong, and what he should do if he is ever in that situation again. Discipline should be done calmly, with logic, and not emotion Discipline is not about intimidation, it is about instruction. Rules and consequences should be consistent- from situation to situation and from child to child. If you are prone to losing your temper with your child, have a written list of steps to go through during the disciplining (teaching) process. Our steps are 1-ask the child what he did that was wrong, 2-discuss with the child WHY it was wrong, 3-talk with the child about what to do differently next time, and 4-have the child apologize and ask for forgiveness. Depending on the misbehavior, sometimes we will precede these steps with a spanking and some room time to think about the misbehavior. If spanking is part of your disciplining process, it should NEVER be delivered in anger.

Create a family history

It seems as though there is always a camera flashing or a video camera recording in our house. We feel that it is extremely important to document the significant moments, as well as the insignificant ones. If you look at our computer, you'll see tens of thousands of pictures- from scanned photos of my wife and I as babies, to my childrens' kindergarten graduations, to the latest wrestle-fest in our living room. The joy of going digital is that all of those photos can be stored on something that doesn't take up a lot of room.

We have several notebooks full of "memoirs"- notes that we have written about our childhoods, as well as our lives growing up, high school memories, college adventures, trips we've taken together, and early marriage. Once our first child came along, the note writing, picture taking, and videoing increased rapidly. We have a notebook full of "kid's notes"- funny or memorable things the kids have done or said over the years. It is fun flipping back through our memoirs, reminding ourselves of all the amazing adventures we've had as a couple and as a family. Individually and as a couple we have overcome many great challenges, and being able to remember those moments allows us to talk to the kids about those times and how it may apply to their lives someday. We can learn as much from our failures as well as our successes. Again, it is important to talk to your kids about your failures, the choices you made, and what you would do differently next time.

Teaching the Keys

As mentioned in the Prepare for Success section, once you and your spouse create your own Keys to a Successful Life, you need to incorporate these into your education plan. Talk to your kids about these Keys whenever the opportunity presents itself. Maya has included some examples below of how we teach the Keys to our children everyday.

Believe in Yourself

We have a motto in our family that we use often- "Travers never give up" My daughter received a jump rope for her birthday one year. She desperately wanted to learn how to use it, so she went out every morning, day after day, but she could not get the hang of it. That weekend, my husband was helping her. He tied knots in the jump rope to shorten it. My daughter kept tripping over the rope, and you could just see the frustration building. She wanted to stop trying and do something else, but my husband reminded her, "Travers never give up!" She persisted, and it paid off...she finally learned how to jump rope that day. My daughter told the story about the first time she remembers truly understanding the words, "Travers never give up!" She was watching my husband chop wood, and he came across a very large, tough piece that was extremely difficult to chop. After trying for some time, my daughter suggested that he give up on that piece of wood and move on. After telling her that Travers never give up, he continued working on that piece of wood, and eventually got it.

All Things in Moderation

It was Halloween night. Kids and candy were spread all over the living room floor. The kids were sorting through and trading candy, and one of them asked, "How much candy can we eat tonight?" Imagine the surprised look on their faces when I replied, "However much you think is reasonable." Believe it or not, they did NOT eat all of their candy in one night. In fact, I heard my older son and his sisters discussing how many pieces were okay to eat that night. At the end of their discussion, they concluded that three or four pieces of candy was a reasonable amount.

Make the Most of Every Opportunity

A few weeks before Christmas our town has a Christmas parade, complete with all sorts of parade floats, the local high school marching band, and various community organizations, include the Cub and Boy Scouts. The first year our son joined the Cub Scouts, we talked with him about marching in the parade. He was really unsure about walking for that distance, without us, and not being able to watch the parade together like we had in past years. We left the decision to our son, but we explained that it is important to make the most of every opportunity. We reminded him that he will have plenty of opportunities in the future to watch parades, but probably very few opportunities to march in parades. He decided to join his Cub Scout pack in the parade, and you should have seen the huge smile on his face when he marched past us, waving happily!

I took my children to a local theater to watch a play about the Wright Brothers. After the play was over, we waited for all of the other school groups to exit the theater, and then went up to the front of the auditorium so I could get some pictures of my kids with the set in the background. The actors heard us talking, and came out from backstage to take pictures with my children. My kids and I talked later about how we had made the most of the opportunity. We took the extra time at the end of the play, and ended up getting some great pictures!

Be Prepared

As we have mentioned before, we love to go camping with our kids. Last summer, while on our camping trip, we decided to hike a nearby mountain. I always pick on my husband for being way over-prepared, but on this particular day I was very thankful that he had prepared so thoroughly. As we were hiking, the rain clouds rolled in, and before we knew it, we were in the middle of a thunderstorm. My husband opened up his backpack and pulled out his tarp and a peanut butter jar full of trail mix. I would not have guessed that we would need a tarp and extra food on our hike, but because he was well prepared he helped make the hike into a positive learning experience for the kids instead of a miserable, cold, wet experience.

Take Personal Responsibility

Show your children that they need to be responsible for their behavior and actions. We were at the doctor's office for our annual checkups, sitting in the waiting room. A lady came in the door, walked over to the check in counter, and said, "I have no idea what time my appointment was. You people didn't call to remind me of my appointment time." My kids and I had a great discussion when we were out of earshot about taking responsibility for your actions. They all agreed that the lady should have written down her appointment time on a calendar, and kept track of it herself.

Think for Yourself

When our kids get into an argument with one another, we think it is important not to solve their problems for them. We have the kids go into a room together, discuss the problem, and come back to us when they have come up with a solution with which they both agree. It is very rare for them to come back to us without a solution, but if they do, we make some suggestions for possible solutions and ask them to decide on the best course of action. It would be a lot easier for us to solve the problem and simply tell the kids what to do, but encouraging them to work on finding a solution teaches them how to work together and think for themselves.

One activity that is extremely popular in our house is building things with Legos, Erector Sets, or Keva planks. It is very rare for our kids to use the step-by-step instructions that come with these toys. Instead, they use their imaginations to build their creations. My son decided one time that he wanted to build a very detailed Lego car, complete with an engine with pistons, a steering wheel with gears, and a battery powered motor to drive the axles. He worked on this car every day for over a week. He had some trouble at times getting things to fit or work properly. A few times he had to take apart a portion of the car and rebuilt it. But he eventually completed the car and was able to drive it around the house. Encouraging the kids to build things without instructions teaches them how to use their imaginations and think for themselves.

Have a Positive Attitude

Your attitude affects everything in your life, and everyone around you. Teach your kids to be grateful for everything, even simple things like sunshine, or a rainy day. We were recently at the doctor's office for our annual checkups. While sitting in the waiting room, a lady came in the door, walked up to the counter to check in, and proceeded to complain about the sun that was streaming in the window into her eyes. A little while later, as my children and I were in the examining room waiting for the doctor, we had a discussion about that lady and her attitude. My kids were astounded that she was complaining about the sun, instead of being grateful for a sunny day!

Be Grateful and Appreciative

A few years ago, we were at a local club for an Easter egg hunt. It was a cool rainy day, and the organizers had planned to have egg hunt outdoors, instead of inside the building as in past years. There was a grandmother there with her young granddaughter, incessantly complaining about the drizzle and the cool weather, and the fact that we had to do this egg hunt outside. Think about what she was teaching her granddaughter! When I heard all of the complaining this woman was doing, I began talking to my children about how we should be grateful that we have the opportunity to participate in a fun egg hunt, that we were getting to spend time together as a family, and that we were able to have some outside time in the crisp, fresh air.

Have Integrity

Respect for other people's things begins in the home. We have a rule that siblings should not play with other siblings' toys without asking. We have a playroom with toys that all the kids are allowed to access. Some of those playroom toys do belong to a particular child, but everyone has access to them because they are in the playroom. Toys that are particularly special to a child are kept in that child's bedroom. Siblings are not allowed to go into another sibling's bedroom without asking. If the door is closed, he or she must knock on the door and not enter unless invited. If these rules are taught and enforced when the kids are young, they will become habits by the time they are teenagers and want more privacy.

Develop Trust and Credibility

Do you ever speak to your kids unkindly? Are you ever impatient with your children? Do you sometimes yell at them when you are frustrated and they are not doing what they are supposed to? I think we all make mistakes when communicating with our children. Once you have made the bad decision, what you do about it teaches your kids how to deal with their bad decisions.

When you make a mistake, it is important that you model the behavior you expect from your children. I recently yelled at my daughter when I walked into her room and the floor was once again covered with paper scraps, markers, scissors, glue, and a lot of other craft supplies. You see, she loves to make things, and earlier that day my toddler had almost stepped on a pair of her open scissors. I had, at that time, explained to her in a calm way that leaving scissors on the floor was dangerous, and I had asked her to clean up all of her supplies. So you can imagine my frustration when I walked into her room and saw all of those items, including the scissors, still on her floor. But instead of maintaining my self-control, I chose to vent my frustration and yell at her. It was when she started crying that I realized my mistake. I immediately apologized to her, and told her that it was wrong of me to yell at her. I explained why I was frustrated, and we talked about what I should have done instead of yelling at her. I then asked for her forgiveness, and told her that in the future I would try hard to maintain self-control and not choose to yell. It took time and effort for me to have that conversation with her, but think about all she learned from that interaction.

Step 4 – Never Stop Improving

How do you know if your family plan is working?
(written by my wife, Maya)

I am with my children close to twenty-four hours a day, seven days a week. I have an hour to myself to do the weekly grocery shopping after dropping the older three kids off at Tae Kwon Do. I sometimes have a little quiet time to myself in the mornings before the kids get up, if I get up early enough! Finally, after getting the kids into bed, I have a little kid-free time before my husband and I collapse into our own bed. You know what? I <u>love</u> being with my children. I sincerely enjoy being around them and am truly grateful that I am able to be home with them all day. When I tell some non-homeschoolers that I get to stay home with my kids all day, I am always shocked and saddened at the response, "I couldn't home school because I couldn't stand to spend that much time with my kids." Sure, sometimes they drive me crazy. Sometimes they choose to do the wrong thing- they disobey, speak unkindly to a sibling, or lose self-control when things don't go their way. But they are such great kids that being around them all the time is a pleasure. They are, for the most part, well behaved, obedient, sweet, caring, fun, and loving children. I think the fact that I love being with them all the time is a strong indication that our plan is working.

Occasionally we go out to eat as a family. Just about every time we are out at a restaurant, people approach our table and comment about how well behaved our children are. One time a mother, clutching onto her noisy toddler, asked me, "How do you get your kids to act like that?" When I take my kids to the library, they walk quietly to the children's' section, instead of running noisily like the other kids. Just today, when I took my son on errands, the secretary in the church office complemented my son on his behavior. My children know how to behave in different situations because we taught them how to do so. We model the correct behavior and we talk about examples of incorrect behavior. My daughter came home from a play date, and she told me about how her friend did not obey when her mom asked her to stop playing and clean up the toys. This observation by my daughter led into a great discussion with all the kids on examples of poor behavior they see in other children. Complements from friends as well as strangers about the good behavior of our children are another indication that our plan is working.

Sometimes I listen in on my kids' conversations with each other. Not in a sneaky way, but like when I am in the kitchen doing dishes, and they are playing and chatting with each other in the next room. It always brings a smile to my face when I hear one of them talking to their siblings like my husband and I would. Recently my younger daughter was attempting to build something out of Legos, and was having some trouble. She started to get fussy and walk away, when my older daughter reminded her of our family motto, "Travers never give up!" She encouraged her younger sibling to keep on trying. My younger daughter continued to work and soon succeeded in building her structure. The words of my older daughter sounded just like what my husband and I would say to our children in that situation. When I hear my children encouraging each other, using words and concepts that my husband and I have taught them, that is an indication that our plan is working.

Never Stop Improving

You've chosen to commit to your child. You and your spouse have worked together and set your goals. You have created your family plan.   You are living your plan by using positive reinforcement and communicating with your child. Structure and accountability have been implemented in your home. You are taking advantage of teaching moments and taking time to involve your kids in all aspects of life. Your family history is complete and you refer to it often when talking to your kids. So now you're done, right? Actually, you have just begun. The mindset of a good leader is always continuous improvement.   You must follow up to make sure your plan is working, and improve upon areas of weakness.

In order for your plans to have credibility you must acknowledge and celebrate the success you achieve. The key is to positively re-enforce the best behavior and figure out how to sustain the gains achieved by your hard work. The areas that aren't quite performing as planned must be identified and talked about. Engage everyone that has responsibility in these areas and work together to drive improvements in these plans. As you achieve successes, adjust your schedule to focus more time on the areas that need more work. In order to sustain processes that are working remember to inspect what you expect or expect nothing at all.

As you go through this process of planning, living out your plan, and continuously improving your plan, remember the goal is to make your life run more smoothly. If you are not seeing the results you want, then you need to re-evaluate your plan and how you are choosing to live out your plan.

Conclusion

While your daily routine likely takes its toll on you, never forget that each day is a gift from God and we need to make the most of it. Life as a parent is definitely not a spectator sport and you will find yourself "tagged in" many times when you had other plans in mind. Always remember that it is the simple things that make life so special and brief everyday moments are often the most enduring memories. Think of your own childhood and what you remember as examples. Think of the stories you hear your elders telling and ask yourself, would these great memories have occurred if the adults in the story hadn't made an effort to make the most of the moment? Find some time to be a great parent each day.

As you have read through the chapters of this book, hopefully you have seen several common themes. These themes come directly from our Keys to a Successful Life document in the appendix. The concepts are simple, but the time and effort to implement them effectively is tremendous. This is why we started out with commitment to our children and to each other. We worked hard to figure out what works and what doesn't and we wanted to share the benefit of our experiences with you. Our hope is that this information helps improve the quality of your life but most of all we hope it helps increase the future potential of your children.

Being a parent is not complicated but it is extremely difficult to do well. To be successful you absolutely must have a plan and a support structure to lean on for help. You must believe in yourself, keep a positive attitude and never lose your sense of humor. Being a parent is one of the greatest blessings you could ever dream of. While you will be challenged in every way (physically, mentally and spiritually) the good times are well worth the price of the hard times.

While you will always be a parent, you have a relatively brief window in time to be a leader for your children. This opportunity will have enormous impact in the development of your children and a corresponding impact on their future potential in life. Remember the good moments from your own childhood and be sure to provide many wonderful moments for your children. The time and effort will be extreme at times, but ask yourself – what do you want your children to remember about you?

You and your spouse will encounter resistance and difficulties in your efforts, but you must know that you are working hard at the goals you have established together and you must rely on each other to be successful. In this way you will find some of the greatest satisfaction that can be found in this life and find yourself much closer to your spouse as a result. I know that writing this book has helped my wife and I get closer, and hopefully it will give you some things to discuss with your spouse.

Most of all remember that life is what you make of it. Do your best every day and never give up. In moments of weakness, look to your spouse and know that together all things are possible.

<u>Appendix</u>

Keys For a Successful Life

Believe in Yourself

- Mindset is Everything
- Be courageous
- Most battles are won or lost in the mind before the first blow is struck
- Whether you believe you can or you can't, you are right
- Trust your instincts
- Be proud of who you are
- Be tough
- Never give up
- Don't accept no or can't as answers
- Stand up for your principles
- Strive for excellence
- Your brain has the majority of influence over your body in most situations
- Stress is the physical result to the brain's inability to handle uncertainty
- Worry is wasted energy (internal friction)
- Experience gives you confidence; confidence is what leaders must project to inspire others to trust in them
- Empowerment happens when people know what you know and feel what you feel.
- Average thinking is for average people, if you want an uncommonly good life then you need to be an uncommonly good decision maker.
- You can't solve big problems by thinking about things

in the same way as you did when the problem occurred.
- If you only do what you have always done you will only get what you have always gotten.

All Things in Moderation

- Balance is the key to most things
- Spend wisely
- Have self-control
- This at the cost of something else
- It is easier to stay healthy than to get health

Make the Most of Every Opportunity

- Hard work beats talent
- Life is not a spectator sport
- Challenge yourself
- Don't wait for things to be offered to you, go find them and earn them
- Take care of the things you own and treat them with respect
- Everything we are today is built on the efforts of our ancestors. What will you contribute to the future?
- The quality of your life is a function of the effort you put into it.

Be Prepared

- Be self reliant
- Knowledge is power
- Security of your family is your responsibility
- Plan ahead
- Always have a back-up plan

Take Personal Responsibility

- You are responsible for your actions and your lack of action
- Recognize every action you take is a choice you make and for which you are responsible
- You are responsible to protect, provide for and prepare your family for success
- In a hero or a goat situation, choose to be the hero, not the goat (there is no in-between)

Think for Yourself

- Observe the world – ask questions
- Gather information – be skeptical
- Decide for yourself
- Do not allow decisions to be made based only on emotions
- Do not allow decisions to be made by default or lack of action
- Make the effort to work through the decision making process, don't be mentally lazy.

- The best decisions are well thought out logic with emotional support (feel good about your logical decisions)
- The key difference between successful people and unsuccessful people is the ability to make good decisions
- If you are not sure, don't

Have a Positive Attitude

- Problems that can be solved with money really aren't that bad
- Happiness is not getting what you want but wanting what you get
- Only you can make yourself happy, decide to be happy
- Problems are only as big as you make them
- Look for positives in everything
- Be optimistic
- Take time to appreciate the many good things in your life, everyday
- Have a sense of humor
- Believe in God and know that He is on your side

Be Grateful and Appreciative

- Show appreciation for what people do for you
- Look for opportunities to give something back
- You reap what you sow
- The best things in life are small everyday events, make the most of them
- Appreciate the things you have and take good care of them

Have integrity

- Be honest
- Keep your promises
- Mean what you say, do what you say
- Treat people and things that belong to other people with respect
- Gain understanding (through communication)

Develop Trust and Credibility

- Keep your promises
- Trust only when you must- trust is earned
- Apologize when you are wrong
- Try to look at things from the other persons point of view
- Be humble
- Use "understanding" for people who are very close to you, consider their comments in context of who they are and how they think.
- Do what you say you will do- In the end, your word is all you have
- As you go through life you gain knowledge & experience that can't be taken away
- All trust and credibility can be lost with one foolish act.
- Say what you mean and mean what you say

Why We Choose to Homeschool

We home school our children so that we can effectively:

1. Empower our children to be self confident about asking questions, using critical thinking skills and making logical decisions vs. peer pressure to conform to popular culture.
2. Teach responsibility, determination, self reliance and the meaning of consequences for their actions.
3. To build self confidence and a network of helpful and supportive friends through social interaction with peers that re-enforces and support Christian conservative values.
4. To benefit from the "one-room school house" effectiveness of having exposure to advanced material before formal expectations begin and to have access to remedial lessons without criticism.
5. Teach life lessons and to apply school lessons to real world scenarios.
6. Teach balance as it applies to time, finances and mindset.
7. To provide learning experiences outside of a classroom environment.
8. To raise academic standards to a globally competitive level, and strive for excellence.
9. To foster a lifelong love of learning by making time to explore concepts that pique curiosity and imagination.
10. To build pride of themselves, their family, the values of the family.
11. To teach thankfulness and appreciation for the opportunities life has presented them.

Morning Routine

Make my bed.
Go to the bathroom and freshen myself.
Get dressed (including socks & shoes if we're going out).
Put my jammies away in my dresser.
Clean my room (choose the messiest horizontal surface).
Do my morning chore (look at the chore board).
Wash my hands (make sure the bathroom is clean while I'm in there).
Meet in the kitchen, ready for breakfast at 7:15 am.
Eat breakfast and vitamin.
Brush my teeth and hair.
Meet in the school room, ready for school at 8:00 am.

Bedtime Routine

Go to the bathroom.
Put on my jammies.
Put my clothes in the hamper or away in my dresser.
Clean my room (choose the messiest horizontal surface).
Lay out my clothes for tomorrow.
Brush my teeth (make sure the bathroom is clean while I'm in there).
Get my bed and water bottle ready.
Meet in the living room for story time.
Say goodnight to Mommy and Daddy.
Get into my bed by 8:30 pm and read.
Turn off my light at my designated bedtime.